Gemstones and Their Origins

Gemstones and Their Origins

Peter C. Keller, Ph.D.

Associate Director
Natural History Museum of Los Angeles County

Featuring Photographs by Harold and Erica Van Pelt
Foreword by Dr. Edward Gübelin

VNR VAN NOSTRAND REINHOLD
_____ New York

Copyright © 1990 by Van Nostrand Reinhold

Library of Congress Catalog Card Number 89-16438
ISBN 0-442-31945-2

Printed in the United States of America

Van Nostrand Reinhold
115 Fifth Avenue
New York, New York 10003

Van Nostrand Reinhold International Company Limited
11 New Fetter Lane
London EC4P 4EE, England

Van Nostrand Reinhold
480 La Trobe Street
Melbourne, Victoria 3000, Australia

Nelson Canada
1120 Birchmount Road
Scarborough, Ontario M1K 5G4, Canada

16   15   14   13   12   11   10   9   8   7   6   5   4   3   2   1

Library of Congress Cataloging-in-Publication Data

Keller, Peter C., 1947–
    Gemstones and their origins / Peter C. Keller ; featuring photographs by Harold and Erica Van Pelt.
        p.   cm.
    Bibliography: p.
    Includes index.
    ISBN 0-442-31945-2
    1. Precious stones.   I. Title.
QE392.K39   1989
553.8—dc20   89-16438
                                                                              CIP

To Elizabeth and Bret, with love

CONTENTS

FOREWORD

Each gem deposit—whether of primary origin in the parent rocks; or secondary as alluvial placers in valley floors, river gravels, or the sand of oceanic shelves—presents an eloquent chronicle of the Earth's life story. It reveals to the expert the prodigious processes which formed the present crust of our planet, of which this volume discloses a small but exciting detail.

The materials of the Earth's crust are the rocks. In this book, the author expounds on how they were formed, why they altered, why they became the cradles of precious gemstones, how they are categorized, and how they are now exploited by man.

What initiates the growth of gemstones? How do they crystallize? Why do gemstones of the same species, originating from different sources, vary? What causes the occurrence of varieties? Why do diamonds, unlike other precious stones, occur not near the Earth's surface in its crust, but deep down beneath it in the upper mantle? These are only a few of the entrancing subjects discussed in this enlightening volume. The reader learns that the Earth is surprisingly alive and altering constantly—sometimes through slow and equable changes and at times by violent and tremendous cataclysms, events from which gemstones issue.

Dr. Peter Keller is certainly to be congratulated on compiling a book about gemstones and their origins. This is a first work of its kind and will be greatly welcomed by all lovers of gemstones. German-speaking gemologists have for decades been privileged by being able to gain detailed knowledge from a comprehensive book* specializing in the detailed description of all varieties of gem deposits, mining and recovery methods, as well as the production of gemstones as far as was known 50 years ago. Yet no book of similar importance was available to the gemological student of the English tongue. In fact, information about the geology of gemstone deposits and the origin of gemstones has in general and until recently been unpardonably neglected in gemological literature and courses. Students of gemology were obliged to learn about the cardinal virtues distinguishing gems from ordinary minerals, and had to memorize enormous quantities of data, yet gained hardly any idea of the geology of the deposits or the geological/petrographical cause of the formation and growth conditions of gemstones.

* O. Stutzer und W. F. Eppler, *DIE LAGERSTAETTEN DER EDEL- UND SCHMUCKSTEINE*, Verlag Gebr. Borntraeger, Berlin, 1935.

Although less universal than the German volume, Dr. Keller's excellent book grants its readers the advantage of a more concise selection and up-to-date description of the geology, mining operations, production, and economy of the most important gem deposits—in some cases referring to historically renowned gems. This volume does justice to the eminent significance of geology in connection with modern gemology. It is now possible for gemologists with a keen interest in the origin of gemstones to find the answers to questions that may have tantalized them before.

On the basis of a modern geological classification, the structure of deposits and their gemstones is excellently defined in this book, offering a clear and easily comprehensible survey of their origin. The list of contents provides the reader with a clear concept of the layout of the book, emphasizing the most important geological events leading to the formation of the different types of deposits which engendered the particularly favorable conditions for gemstone crystallization. Thus the reader is informed how gemstones are the products of various completely different happenings in and beneath the Earth's crust.

Knowledge of the geology of gem deposits has recently become more vital for a complete understanding of gemstones and their distinction from synthetics than knowledge of many of their other properties so highly assessed heretofore. The relatively confined realm of gemstones encompasses a domain in which all geological formations may be encountered. Consequently, the study of the origin of gemstones is simultaneously a comprehensive introduction to geology. In addition, the investigation of inclusions—fluid as well as solid—has contributed remarkably towards a better and sometimes even a decisive understanding of the origin and growth stages of gemstones in certain geological environments.

This volume offers fascinating reading for the well-informed gemologist, at the same time rendering the beginner more familiar with the essential secrets of the gemstones' origins. Quite often, one gains the impression that one is actually present in a described deposit; observing how the gem crystals grow in their birth chambers, or watching the miners at their arduous yet exciting work.

The text certainly inspires the reader not only to learn all about the origin of gemstones but also to observe, to prospect, to conclude, and especially to marvel. One learns that the study of gem deposits and their formation is a fascinating science. In addition to the highly elucidating text, the volume is superbly illustrated; imparting to the reader a vivid impression of the appearance of many gem minerals and their modes of exploitation, and transporting one into the fabulous world of gemstones. Dr. Keller's book is truly indispensible to any student of gemology, graduate gemologist, jeweler and jewelry sales staff, and is earnestly recommended to mineralogists, collectors, and especially to all lovers of gemstones.

Dr. Edward Gübelin
Meggen, Switzerland

PREFACE

A few years ago, I was approached by a gentleman who surprised me by stating that gemstones did not belong in a natural history museum. He went on to say that gemstones were minerals that had been worked by an artisan, and as such, told us nothing of our earth's history. They would be much more appropriate in an art museum, or if the gems had historical importance, they could be placed in a history museum, but under no circumstance was a faceted gemstone appropriate to natural history. This argument initially startled me since next to dinosaurs, gemstones are among the most popular objects sought out by visitors to many of the world's natural history museums. But after some thought, I realized that the challenger was to a large extent correct. In most natural history museums gemstones are displayed as beautiful objects, much as they would be in a jewelry store, with little or no information about their relevance to earth history. Furthermore, literature on the subject is widely dispersed, and often very difficult to find. The response to the above challenge was a gallery in the Natural History Museum of Los Angeles County, entitled "Gemstones and Their Origins," which opened in 1985, thanks to the generosity of Alex Deutsch.

The purpose of this book is to expand on the idea initially proposed in the museum exhibit and to include data that I have collected as a result of my interest in gem occurrences. Much of this information was collected on frequent trips to gem deposits, and published in various journals, especially *Gems & Gemology*. The book is divided into four parts based on geologic processes taking place at increasingly greater depth below the earth's surface. Each geologic process is examined, in detail, along with an example of an important gem deposit where this process has been observed. In each chapter, other deposits of a similar nature will also be discussed briefly, although important references from the literature will be included for any reader interested in more information.

Part I of the book examines those geologic processes responsible for the development of gemstones deposited by water on the earth's surface. These are considered sedimentary deposits. This first part is subdivided into two chapters.

The first chapter examines deposits of gemstones in which the previously formed gemstones are reconcentrated into important deposits by surface waters. The classic gem gravels of Sri Lanka are used as an example of one of these secondary or alluvial deposits. The second chapter discusses the chemically precipitated gemstones created through the agency of surface waters, focusing on the opal deposits of Australia.

Part II of this book is devoted to those gem deposits formed by molten rock and related hydrothermal fluids. It is subdivided into three chapters: hydrothermal deposits, with the emeralds of Colombia as an example; the pegmatites of Minas Gerais, Brazil; and those gemstones formed in a magma at depth and brought to the earth's surface as a volcano or fissure eruption, which describes the rubies of Chanthaburi-Trat, Thailand.

As we go deeper into the earth's crust, we encounter metamorphic deposits which can be divided quite broadly into low-pressure deposits and high-pressure deposits. In Part III, we examine these deposits. The chapter discussing gemstones formed by low-pressure regional metamorphism examines the famous ruby deposits of Mogok, Burma. This is an admittedly controversial chapter, since many textbooks state that Mogok is of "contact" metamorphic origin. No such evidence has been cited in the literature, however, that couldn't equally well be applied to low-pressure regional metamorphism. High-pressure regional metamorphism gem deposits are rare, but are discussed in the context of the jadeite deposits of northern Burma.

Our descent into the earth's crust ends in Part IV at the base of the crust and in the earth's upper mantle, some 100 miles below the earth's surface. Here, in this very-high-pressure, high-temperature environment two very special gemstones, peridot and diamond, are produced. These rare glimpses of the earth's mantle are brought to the surface in "mantle thrust sheets" and a rare type of volcano known as a "pipe," respectively. The classic peridot of Zabargad Island, Egypt and the new find at Argyle in Western Australia are used as examples. It is worth noting that the Argyle pipe was unknown until 1980; but since its first full-scale year of production in 1986, it has become the number one producer of diamonds in the world, producing 30,000,000 carats in that first year.

This book examines most of the major geologic processes responsible for the formation of gemstones, and in doing so, reviews what is known about nine classic gem deposits. We hope that it will spur further interest in these deposits, and can act as a catalyst to examination of the many deposits that have not been highlighted here. Gemstones do reveal a great deal about Earth history, especially because they usually represent minerals in their purest form. Because they are also unusually durable, they withstand the rigors of the geologic processes that take place after their formation when other minerals do not. They often are protective vehicles for small inclusions of liquids, gases, or other minerals that tell us a great deal about remote geologic conditions that otherwise would not be obtainable. Gemstones are very important artifacts of natural history.

ACKNOWLEDGMENTS

This book would not have been possible without the generous assistance of a great number of friends and associates. The initial concept, which resulted in a permanent exhibition at the Natural History Museum of Los Angeles County, would not have been possible without the encouragement and generous support of Alex Deutsch and Dr. Giles Mead. Dr. Anthony Kampf is a stimulating colleague who was instrumental in the development of the *Gemstones and Their Origins* concept. Dr. John Sinkankas was particularly encouraging in the transformation of the original exhibit concept to book form. He has subsequently been a tremendous help in reviewing major segments of the manuscript. Very special thanks must also go to Dr. Edward Gübelin for his encouragement, advice, and substantial editing. He was also very generous with his photo library.

Individuals who are far more familiar than I with specific gem-producing regions or aspects of the geologic processes responsible for their formation reviewed appropriate chapters. Dr. Pieter Zwaan, Director of the National Museum of Geology and Mineralogy in Leiden, the Netherlands, examined the chapter on alluvial deposits and Sri Lanka. Dr. Ralph Segnit, Chairman of the Committee for Gem Materials of the International Mineralogical Association and associated with the CSIRO Division of Mineral Chemistry at Port Melbourne, Australia gave invaluable input into the chapter on Australian opal deposits. The chapter on Colombian emeralds was reviewed by Dr. John Sinkankas. Dr. Alan Jobbins of the Gemmological Association of Great Britain was a tremendous help in obtaining information on the Burmese jadeite deposits. Dr. Henry Meyer of Purdue University and Dr. James Shigley of the Gemological Institute of America reviewed the chapter on Australian diamonds. Ray Sparvell of Argyle Diamonds, Ltd., provided invaluable information on the Argyle deposit. Special thanks goes to Dr. Art Montana, Chairman of the Department of Earth and Planetary Sciences at UCLA for his encouragement and review of major segments of the manuscript, as well as for providing me with access to the UCLA geology library. Robin Walker of DeBeers Consolidated Mines, Ltd., should also be thanked for his input and advice on diamonds.

Photographs are a very important part of this book, and very special thanks must be given to Harold and Erica Van Pelt for their constant and very generous support. They were always willing to help, not only with a great number of superb photographs but also with advice when it was most needed. Spectacular photographs of Sri Lanka were provided by Peter Horree of the Netherlands. The family of the late Dr. John Sanders, formerly of the University of Melbourne, provided the TEM photomicrographs of opal. The South Australia Department of Mines and Energy provided the photographs of Australian opal mining. Photographs of Zabargad Island were generously provided by Dr. Peter Bancroft, and Rock Currier opened up his slide library to provide slides of significant Zabargad peridot specimens. Argyle Diamond Sales, Ltd., was responsible for photographs of the Argyle mine and the spectacular pink diamond. The Smithsonian Institution, particularly John Sampson White, Associate Curator of Mineralogy, provided numerous photographs of gems from its collections.

Finally, no project such as this is possible without the understanding support of the editors, assistants, and graphic artists. Very special thanks must go to Peggy Zeadow, who typed many drafts of this manuscript and generally kept me organized in the process, and to Mary Butler for all the hours she spent over the drafting table.

ABOUT THE ILLUSTRATIONS

The photographic team of Harold and Erica Van Pelt is synonymous with some of the world's finest gem and mineral photography. They have traveled extensively throughout the world to visit and photograph famous mines, major museum collections, as well as some of the world's finest private gem and mineral collections. Their photographs have appeared in almost every important gem and mineral magazine. Most of the covers for *Gems & Gemology* magazine have been provided by the Van Pelts. The Van Pelts have also made major contributions to over half a dozen books on gems and minerals, including *The Gem Collection of the Smithsonian; Brazil, Paradise of Gemstones; Emerald and Other Beryls; Gemstones of North America;* and *Gem and Crystal Treasures.*

In addition to being superb photographers, they are true connoisseurs of fine gem and mineral specimens, jewelry designers, and classic lapidaries. They truly know and love their subject.

Many of the locality photographs have been taken by the author on his trips to study the gem deposits. Others, such as those provided by Dr. Edward Gübelin are of localities that are no longer accessible and are, therefore, especially rare. Many of the photographs have never before been published.

PART I

Gemstones Deposited by Water on the Earth's Surface

1

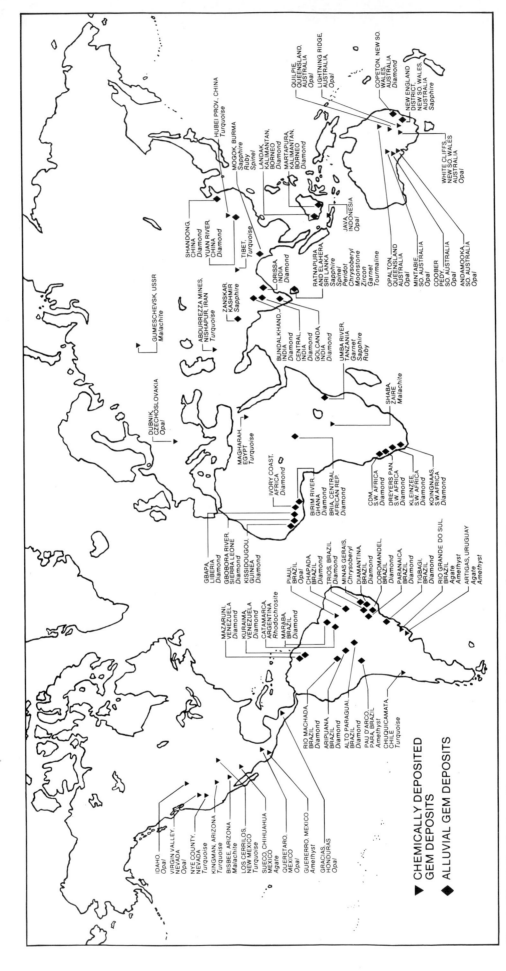

Map 1. *World distribution of important gem deposits formed by surface waters.*

Labels on map:

HUBEI PROV., CHINA
Turquoise

QUILPIE, QUEENSLAND, AUSTRALIA
Opal

LIGHTNING RIDGE, AUSTRALIA
Opal

COPETON, NEW SO. WALES, AUSTRALIA
Diamond

NEW ENGLAND DISTRICT, NEW SO. WALES, AUSTRALIA
Sapphire

MOGOK, BURMA
Sapphire
Ruby
Spinel

LANDAK, KALIMANTAN, BORNEO
Diamond

MARTAPURA, KALIMANTAN, BORNEO
Diamond

WHITE CLIFFS, NEW SO. WALES, AUSTRALIA
Opal

SHANDONG, CHINA
Diamond

YUAN RIVER, CHINA
Diamond

TIBET, *Turquoise*

ORISSA, INDIA
Diamond

RATNAPURA AND ELAHERA, SRI LANKA
Sapphire
Spinel
Peridot
Chrysoberyl
Moonstone
Zircon
Garnet
Tourmaline

JAVA, INDONESIA
Opal

OPALTON, QUEENSLAND, AUSTRALIA
Opal

ABDURREZZA MINES, NISHAPUR, IRAN
Turquoise

ZANSKAR, KASHMIR
Sapphire

BUNDALKHAND, INDIA
Diamond

CENTRAL INDIA
Diamond

GOLCANDA, INDIA
Diamond

UMBA RIVER, TANZANIA
Garnet
Sapphire
Ruby

MINTABIE, SO. AUSTRALIA
Opal

COOBER PEDY, SO. AUSTRALIA
Opal

ANDAMOOKA, SO. AUSTRALIA
Opal

GUMESCHEVSK, USSR
Malachite

DUBNIK, CZECHOSLOVAKIA
Opal

MAGHARAH, EGYPT
Turquoise

SHABA, ZAIRE
Malachite

IVORY COAST, AFRICA
Diamond

BIRIM RIVER, GHANA
Diamond

BRIA, CENTRAL AFRICAN REP.
Diamond

GBAPA, LIBERIA
Diamond

GBOBORA RIVER, SIERRA LEONE
Diamond

KISSIDOUGOU, GUINEA
Diamond

CDM, S.W. AFRICA
Diamond

DREYERS PAN, S.W. AFRICA
Diamond

KLEINZEE, S.W. AFRICA
Diamond

KOINGNAAS, S.W. AFRICA
Diamond

PIAUI, BRAZIL
Opal

CHAPADA, BRAZIL
Diamond

TRIOS, BRAZIL
Diamond

MINAS GERAIS, BRAZIL
Chrysoberyl

DIAMANTINA, BRAZIL
Diamond

COROMANDEL, BRAZIL
Diamond

PARANAICA, BRAZIL
Diamond

TIGBAGI, BRAZIL
Diamond

RIO GRANDE DO SUL, BRAZIL
Agate

ARTIGAS, URUGUAY
Amethyst

MAZARUNI, VENEZUELA
Diamond

KURAIMA, VENEZUELA
Diamond

CATAMARCA, ARGENTINA
Rhodochrosite

MARABA, BRAZIL
Diamond

RIO MACHADA, BRAZIL
Diamond

ARIPUANA, BRAZIL
Diamond

ALTO PARAGUAI, BRAZIL
Diamond

PAU D'ARCO, PARA, BRAZIL
Amethyst

CHUQUICAMATA, CHILE
Turquoise

IDAHO
Opal

VIRGIN VALLEY, NEVADA
Opal

NYE COUNTY, NEVADA
Turquoise

KINGMAN, ARIZONA
Turquoise

BISBEE, ARIZONA
Malachite

LOS CERRILOS, NEW MEXICO
Turquoise

SUECO, CHIHUAHUA, MEXICO
Agate

QUERETARO, MEXICO
Opal

GUERERRO, MEXICO
Amethyst

GRACIAS, HONDURAS
Opal

▶ CHEMICALLY DEPOSITED GEM DEPOSITS

◆ ALLUVIAL GEM DEPOSITS

2

*W*ater plays an important role in the formation of gem deposits at or near the surface of the earth. Over millions of years, rocks exposed on the earth's surface crumble under the destructive forces of the earth's atmosphere: Wind, rain, snow, and ice all contribute to weathering, the slow, steady disintegration of rocks. With age, the jagged peaks of a young mountain range become rounded and eventually are leveled to mere bumps on the landscape. The minerals that are the building blocks of the rocks that make up these mountains break down over time to different degrees and in different ways. Certain physical properties of the mineral, such as cleavage and hardness, determine the ability of any given mineral to withstand such break down. Many minerals simply fracture into smaller and smaller fragments until they become sandlike grains, and some minerals dissolve completely and are swept away in the water of streams and rivers.

Over millennia, billions of tons of rock weather and erode, but some minerals in these crumbling rocks resist both mechanical and chemical breakdown. They are heavier than other minerals, and in water they tend to sink faster and thus travel less far. These durable and heavy minerals are thereby concentrated anywhere that rivers or streams slow and allow them to drop to the streambed. Such rapid settling of very heavy minerals is typical of gold and platinum, which sometimes are referred to as the noble metals *because of their seemingly indestructible nature. Being very heavy, they commonly concentrate in riverbeds to form what are called* placer deposits. *Certain gemstones, notably diamonds, rubies, sapphires, topazes, spinels, tourmalines, jade, aquamarines, and chrysoberyls, although not nearly as heavy, are also durable and dense and form similar placer deposits. Today, more gemstones are mined from ancient riverbeds than from any other type of deposit.*

Water plays an entirely different role when it dissolves minerals. We seldom think of ordinary water as capable of dissolving rock, but, given sufficient time, particularly if the water is acidic or basic or has been heated, it readily dissolves many kinds of minerals. Water contributes directly to the formation of minerals through chemical reaction, evaporation, or cooling of heated water. When water carrying dissolved minerals encounters proper conditions underground or other minerals with which it can react, it deposits new minerals in seams, cavities, and other open spaces. Gemstones that may be formed in this way include turquoise, malachite, amethyst, rhodochrosite, and opal, the most valued of this group of gems (Map 1).

1

Gemstones Concentrated by Surface Waters:
The Gem Gravels of Sri Lanka

When gemstones are hard and tough enough to withstand mechanical breakdown, chemically resistant to attack by natural acids or bases, and dense enough to be concentrated, they can form secondary placer or alluvial deposits. Diamonds, rubies, sapphires, jades, tourmalines, topazes, spinels, aquamarines, and chrysoberyls are but a few of the minerals that may be freed from the softer parent rock by weathering, eroded and transported down a slope to the nearest stream, and further carried along by river currents and/or wave action. Moving stream water sweeps away the lighter minerals, and the heavier placer minerals, such as diamond and corundum, sink to the bottom or are moved downstream a relatively short distance. Waves and shore currents also separate heavy minerals from lighter ones and coarse grains from finer ones. From thousands of tons of debris, the few heavy mineral grains in each ton of rock are gradually concentrated in the stream or beach gravels until they accumulate in sufficient abundance to be worth mining.

The river's ability to carry these relatively heavy mineral grains depends primarily on the velocity of the water (Fig. 1-1). Where a stream naturally slows, gemstones are deposited and, in time, concentrated much the same way as gold in a California Forty-Niner's swirling gold pan. If the water velocity is too low, the lighter minerals are not removed. If the water moves too fast, however, the heavier placer gems are swept away and perhaps dissipated. A slackening of the stream's velocity causes deposition and accumulation. In a stream, a change in gradient, meander, spreading, or obstruction in the streambed can produce the reduced velocity that permits heavier minerals to drop and accumulate. Stream water may start out in the mountains rushing through canyons and sweeping everything along with it. The stream velocity slackens in wide places, swirls around the outside of bends in the channel, and creates back eddies on the inside of the bend that allow heavier minerals to drop. Elsewhere in the streambed, natural irregularities called *riffles* may form in alter-

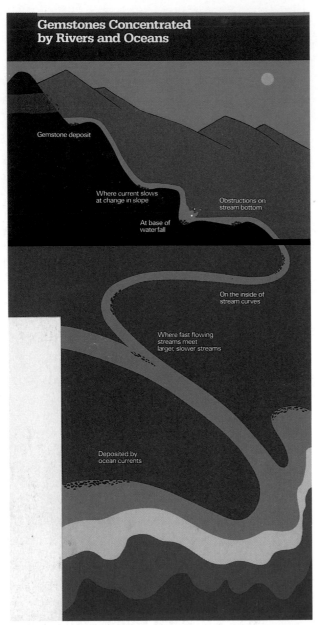

Gemstones Concentrated by Rivers and Oceans

Gemstone deposit

Where current slows
at change in slope

Obstructions on
stream bottom

At base of
waterfall

On the inside of
stream curves

Where fast flowing
streams meet
larger, slower streams

Deposited by
ocean currents

Figure 1-1. Diagram showing slowing of stream waters to allow for the formation of alluvial deposits. Courtesy of the Natural History Museum of Los Angeles County.

nating hard and soft layers of slates, schists, and other layered rocks. Such natural riffles are excellent traps for placer gems and may give rise to exceedingly rich deposits (Guilbert and Park, 1986).

In placer deposits, the gemstones are typically sorted by size and density. Thousands of tons of rock may yield only a few gemstones in these stream gravels. Because of the rough treatment they endured, however, the gems found concentrated in placer deposits are of much finer quality than those found in the primary deposit or parent rock. The abrasion and pounding along the streambed eliminates flawed or weaker areas of the gemstone and leaves a much higher quality stone in the final concentrate. Diamonds illustrate this point well. Generally speaking, only about 10 percent of the diamonds recovered from kimberlite pipes are of gem quality. In placer deposits, however, almost 90 percent of the diamonds recovered are of gem quality because the weaker stones have been destroyed in transit.

Gem-bearing alluvial deposits are found throughout the world. The diamondiferous beach sands on either side of the mouth of the Orange River in South Africa and Namibia represent millions of years of weathering and erosion of kimberlites and are the richest placer diamond deposits in the world (Webster, 1975; Wilson, 1948). Brazil has important placer diamond deposits in Minas Gerais, particularly near Diamantina, various areas in Bahia, the Corrutela and Araguaia regions of Mato Grosso, and the Gibue's district in Piauí. Placer diamonds are also found in several river systems in Guyana and Venezuela. Among the world's oldest and most famous diamond mines are placer deposits along the eastern edge of the Deccan Plateau in India, including the Golconda mines in the Central district of Maharashtra, and also in the Eastern district in Orissa and the Bundelkhand (Northern) district in Madhya Pradesh. This latter district includes the famous Panna mines (Scalisi and Cook, 1983).

The oldest diamond mines are thought to be in Indonesia, the Sungai Landak placer deposits in western Kalimantan (Borneo) and the placer swamp deposits just west of Martapura in southeastern Kalimantan (Spencer et al., 1988). Other placer or alluvial diamond deposits are found in China, particularly in the Yüan River in Hunan, and in west and central African countries.

Many of the world's finest gem rubies and sapphires came from placer deposits located not far from their parent rock source near Mogok in northern Burma (Keller, 1983) and the Umba River of northeastern Tanzania (Zwaan, 1974; Webster, 1961). Northern Burma also produces the world's finest jadeite, in part from important placer deposits in the Uru River valley at Hpakant. Many of the world's pegmatite regions have placer deposits associated with them. Proctor (1984) discusses the important aspects of the placer mining of pegmatite gems in Minas Gerais, Brazil. Interestingly enough, emerald is too delicate to withstand the rigors of stream transport and is never found as a placer mineral, but some has been found as crystals weathered from outcrops of emerald-bearing rocks.

THE GEM GRAVELS OF SRI LANKA

The most prolific and diverse of all placer deposits are found on the tropical island of Sri Lanka (formerly Ceylon), without doubt, one of the most important gemstone regions in the world. Its area is about that of West Virginia, and it is situated in the Indian Ocean off the southeastern coast of India. It has commonly been called the "island of gems" because of the large and spectacular array of gems it has produced for many centuries. No other gem locality in the world has been so important for so much of recorded history. Sri Lanka's gem gravels, known locally as *illam*, are best known for their fine sapphires, which display a huge array of colors (Fig. 1-2). However, the rich gravels also yield rounded pebbles of the cat's-eye and alexandrite varieties of chrysoberyl (Fig. 1-3), ruby, garnet, spinel, zircon, peridot, tourmaline, beryl, moonstone, and many lesser known, rare gem species (Fig. 1-4). Ironically, the parent rock of these gemstones remains uncertain but is undoubtedly somewhere in the extensive Precambrian metamorphic sequence that makes up over 90 percent of the island.

Figure 1-3. Blue star sapphires and fine cat's eye chrysoberyl are among the most prized of Sri Lanka's gemstones. Photo by Harold and Erica Van Pelt.

Figure 1-2. Sri Lanka is best known for its sapphires. Although sapphire is most commonly thought to be blue, it actually occurs in almost any color, as illustrated in this photograph of sapphires from the Hixon Collection of the Natural History Museum of Los Angeles County. Photo by Harold and Erica Van Pelt.

Figure 1-4. These gem spinels, ranging from 6 to 55 carats, illustrate some of the many colors of spinel found in Sri Lankan gem gravels. Stones from the Hixon Collection of the Natural History Museum of Los Angeles County. Photo by Harold and Erica Van Pelt.

Although gem deposits are found throughout central and southern Sri Lanka, large-scale mining activity is confined mainly to the Ratnapura and Elahera areas. Ratnapura, the "city of gems," is located approximately 97 km southeast of the capital city of Colombo and is, along with the surrounding area in Sabaragamuwa Province, the major gem-producing area on the island. The gems are found in certain horizons in river and lake deposits that have accumulated to a thickness of about 10 to 15 meters in the valley bottoms. The gemstones are usually found in the lowest gravels and sands overlying weathered bedrock. In the last 20 years the Elahera area, located about 115 km northeast of Colombo in Central Province, has grown in importance to become the second largest producer of gems in Sri Lanka. An estimated 35 percent of the gemstones exported from Sri Lanka now come from the Elahera area (Gunawardene and Rupasinghe, 1986). The Elahera gem field covers approximately 150 square km in the Matale and Polonnaruwa districts of Central Province. Most mining activity is along the Kalu Ganga, a major tributary of the island's longest river, the Mahaweli Ganga. Access to the area is limited to the dry season, and access permits must be obtained from the State Gem Corporation, which totally controls the area. Less important mining areas in Sri Lanka include Okkampitiya and Tissamaharama. The gem deposits of Sri Lanka have been studied in great detail over the last century. The most important works on the subject include Lacroix (1891), Hapuarachehi (1960), Wadia and Fernando (1945), Adams (1929), Gübelin (1968), Zwaan (1982), Herath (1982), and Gunawardene and Rupasinghe (1986). Their studies include general descriptions of the island's geology, the nature of the gem occurrences, and questions regarding the source of the island's gemstones.

History

Detailed descriptions of the mining history of Sri Lanka are almost nonexistent. However, brief written references to the gems of the island through much of historic time, together with major Sri Lankan gems in many ancient treasuries, point to the great importance of the island for at least 2,500 years. According to Perera (1939) reference was made in the Scriptures to gems brought from Ceylon to the court of Solomon. Bancroft (1984) states that in 500 B.C. Buddhists from northern India conquered the island and began mining and setting gems into jewelry for trade abroad. Certainly, royal treasures from all over the world, from the crown jewels of Great Britain to the Ming Dynasty tombs

and the treasures of the Forbidden City of China, all boast a wealth of Sri Lanka's gemstones. According to Zwaan (1982), one of the earliest descriptions of mining in Sri Lanka is that of Nearchus, Alexander the Great's celebrated admiral, who in 334 B.C. mentioned an island not far from Persia where beautiful translucent gems were found. According to Bancroft (1984), Marco Polo wrote of his 1292 visit: "I want you to understand that the island of Ceylon is, for its size, the finest island in the world, and from its streams come rubies, sapphires, topazes, amethyst, and garnet." Gunawardene and Rupasinghe (1986) reported that during Marco Polo's time the Elahera area was being mined extensively, particularly by foreigners, although this particular area was later abandoned and not rediscovered until hundreds of years later. In the mid-1940s, an engineer digging an irrigation ditch accidentally rediscovered the Elahera deposit. Mining began immediately, but not until the late 1970s, when the newly formed State Gem Corporation set up a large-scale effort, did mining activity in the Elahera area become significant. Today approximately 650 miners work in the area under the control of the State Gem Corporation.

Geology of Sri Lanka

The island of Sri Lanka is primarily a part of the large shield area that comprises peninsular India. The area was apparently geologically stable over a very long period of time. In Tertiary times, however, the northwestern part of the island, including the Jaffna peninsula, submerged, and deposition of Miocene sediments resulted. A look at a geologic map of Sri Lanka reflects this relatively simple history (Fig. 1-5). Except for a narrow band of Miocene limestones and calcareous sandstones on the island's northwestern coast, Sri Lanka is underlain entirely by regionally metamorphosed Precambrian rocks and intrusive granites. These rocks, believed to be a geological continuation of the Archaean complex of southern India, were divided by Fernando (1948) into the khondalite series of paragneisses and associated granitic intrusions and the underlying orthogneisses and paragneisses of the Vijayan series. More recently, Cooray (1967) eliminated the name *khondalite* and subdivided Sri Lanka's Precambrian rocks into three major units: (1) the Highland series, which is basically Fernando's (1948) khondalite series and consists of garnetiferous gneisses with charnockites, quartzites, marbles, and granulites; (2) the Vijayan series, which consists of hornblende-biotite gneisses and associated granites; and (3) the Southwestern group of cordierite, hypersthene, and sil-

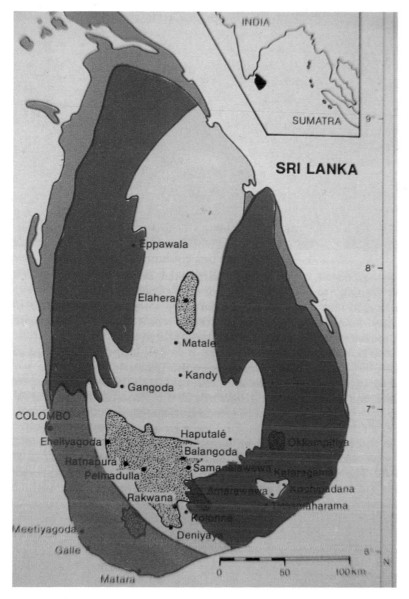

Figure 1-5. Geologic sketchmap of Sri Lanka, with geologic units colored and the main gem-producing areas identified with a strippled pattern. The geologic units include the Southwest group (green), the Vijayan complex (red), and the Highland group (yellow)—all of Precambrian age. The much younger Cenozoic sediments are shown in blue and are limited to the northern two-thirds of the island's coastline (Zwaan, 1982). Courtesy of the Gemological Institute of America.

limanite gneisses. The Highland series is of greatest interest gemologically, for it is generally believed to be the most likely source for many of Sri Lanka's gemstones. Furthermore, almost all of the Ratnapura and Elahera gem fields are underlain by rocks of this series.

As with any significant placer gem deposits, the original source for Sri Lanka's gem riches has been the subject of extensive research and great debate (Dahanayake, 1980; Gunaratne, 1976; Katz, 1969; Katz, 1971; Munasinghe and Dissanayake, 1981). Finding the parent rock is interesting to the scientist, but very important economically to the gem industry. Adams (1929) believed that the gem minerals were derived from the nearby and underlying crystalline rocks of what is now designated as the Highland series. After summarizing the devel-

opment of concepts concerning the source of Sri Lanka's gems and studying the cordierite gneisses of the Southwestern group, Katz (1972) concluded that the unit could be a source: "the distinctive paragenesis of the cordierite gneisses suggest[s] that they are a possible source rock for many of the gem deposits on the island." Of course, further contributions from pegmatites would supply the beryl, moonstone, tourmaline, topaz, and other typical pegmatitic minerals. In this connection Coates (1935) and Wadia and Fernando (1945) urged a pegmatitic origin for all of Sri Lanka's gemstones, but their theory has been discounted on geochemical grounds as well as the sheer lack of a potential supply from the relatively minor pegmatite deposits of the area to account for the major gem deposits observed. Silva (1976) suggests that the garnetiferous gneisses of the Highland series are the most likely sources because of their close proximity to the overlying gravels and because of geochemical considerations. The most convincing proof of parent rock for Sri Lanka's gemstones obviously would be gemstones in situ, and numerous attempts to locate the parent rock have been made during this century. To date, five minor localities of corundum and/or spinel have been identified.

Coomaraswamy (1903) was the first to locate sapphire in situ on the island when he found opaque, nongem crystal in a thin band of decomposed feldspathic granulite near Kandy. In the following year he located on the Haldummula Estate near Haputale fallen blocks of a corundum-sillimanite rock with tabular blue prisms of corundum. A third in situ occurrence of corundum was described by Coates (1935) who found hexagonal crystals up to 2.5 cm long associated with feldspar and biotite in a narrow zone bordering a pegmatite dike in decomposed granulite at Aparekka near Matara. Wells (1956) found in situ gemmy blue corundum near the Non Pareil Estate at Ohiya. The crystals occur on the micaceous margins of a band of crystalline limestone and a syenite. Wells also found mauve spinel with the corundum and concluded that the corundum was the result of desilication of the syenite magma by limestone. In the late 1950s, Cooray and Kumarapeli (1960) found corundum as isolated porphyroblasts in a gneiss near Gangodo and considered the host rocks to be almost identical to those described by Coomaraswamy (1903) but originating from the metamorphosed equivalents of silica-poor sediments. Gunaratne (1976) found corundum in Kolonne.

Gemstone Occurrences

Typical Sri Lankan gem gravels are lens-shaped, generally a few centimeters to almost a meter in thickness, and are located from 2 to 15 meters below the surface. The most abundant constituent is quartz in the form of well-rounded pebbles.

Dahanayake, Liyanage, and Ranasinghe (1980) provided a detailed study of sediments in 30 gem pits at Ratnapura and Elahera to determine the modes of occurrence of the gem-bearing gravels and possible sources of the gem minerals. Both areas are characterized by ridge-and-valley topography, with the valley floors covered with unconsolidated alluvials underlain by Highland series rocks, mainly garnetiferous gneisses and granulite, with rare occurrences of marbles and pegmatites.

The pits in the valley floor tend to be very wet, whereas those found on the ridge slopes are dry and easier to study. Dahanayake, Liyanage, and

Ranasinghe (1980) classified the gem-bearing placer gravels into three types: (1) residual, (2) eluvial, and (3) alluvial. They determined that the residual, which consisted of gem minerals that were mostly deposited in situ, ranged in depth from a few centimeters to about 10 meters below the surface. These pits consisted mostly of angular rock fragments lying on top of weathered garnetiferous gneisses.

The eluvial beds contained minerals transported only short distances along the slopes of ridges and were deposited close to the parent rock. These beds usually were found exposed on the surface and consisted of slightly rounded rock fragments lying on weathered garnetiferous gneisses.

The alluvial beds contained gem materials that were transported along streams and were deposited at great distances from parent rocks. These beds were found at depths up to 15 meters below the surface in ancient stream channels, and the rock fragments were typically rounded as a result of transport.

The majority of gem minerals found in all beds were blue and pink sapphires and blue spinels. Dahanayake, Liyanage, and Ranasinghe (1980) concluded that the corundum and spinels were both derived from garnetiferous gneisses, and localized skarn deposits, white topaz, beryl, tourmaline, and chrysoberyl may have come from the localized pegmatites.

Mining Techniques

The method of gemstone recovery has remained unchanged for centuries. Before digging, a long pole is driven into the ground to determine how deep the gem gravel *(illam)* lies. If it is found only a few feet below the surface, a simple circular pit is sunk to the gem layer, but if the gravel is deeper, a vertical shaft with timbered sides must be constructed (Fig. 1-6). Due to the prevailing shallow water table, the shaft quickly floods and pumping or bailing is required almost continually.

As the shaft deepens, palm-planked scaffolding must be built, and the walls must be reinforced with palm leaves (Fig. 1-7). The only tools are a pick, shovel, spade, and basket. The basket is filled with mud and passed up and out of the pit and then returned for more. When the pit becomes too deep for baskets, the mud and water are pulleyed to the surface in cans.

When the gem gravel layer is reached, the gravel is taken from the pit or shaft and washed in a large round basket known as a *watti* (Fig. 1-8). The watti duplicates nature's concentrating method. As

Figure 1-6. View down a mine shaft in Sri Lanka. Photo by P. Horree.

Figure 1-7. In Sri Lanka, hand-operated hoists are often used to lift buried gem gravel (known as illam) to the surface. Here, a vertical shaft has been dug through many feet of overburden to reach the illam containing sapphire, cat's-eye chrysoberyl, spinel, and many less-known gems. Photo by P. Horree.

Figure 1-8. Washing of the illam in Ratnapura, Sri Lanka. Photo by P. Horree.

Figure 1-9. Hand-dredging the riverbed for gem gravels in Sri Lanka. Photo by P. Horree.

the miner swirls water in the basket, the lighter sand and mud are washed away, leaving behind the heavier pebbles.

After the washing, the basket is turned over to the sorter, usually the most experienced miner, who quickly but thoroughly inspects the gem concentrate.

Mining gravels from present-day riverbeds requires dredging, a technique now much employed in many areas of central and southern Sri Lanka, especially the Kelani Ganga and the Kalu Ganga. To prepare for dredging, miners erect a brush dam wherever the stream naturally slows and thus concentrates gem minerals or where streams are dammed and the water is forced to flow faster over the wooden dams. They then dig a ditch just upstream from the dam. In the fast-moving river water, the miners use long-handled scrapers called

mamoti to scoop up the gravel from the riverbed, deposit it in the ditch, and allow the fast-moving dam water to remove the small and lighter minerals from the gem concentrate (Fig. 1-9). The concentrate is then placed into the circular basket used throughout Sri Lanka for further panning that leaves a high-grade concentrate of gem gravel. Then the sorter takes over and looks for the glistening gemstone pebbles (Gübelin, 1968).

Today, under the auspices of the State Gem Corporation, large-scale surface mining has been initiated. Overburden is scraped off with bulldozers to expose the gem gravels. The gem gravels are still washed by hand in the traditional round baskets, however, and sorted and dried in the sun for a final hand sorting to recover any gem material that was overlooked in the washing operation (Dissanayake, 1981).

Famous Gems from Sri Lanka

Gunawardene and Rupasinghe (1986) record peak annual gem exports from Sri Lanka in 1980 at more than $40 million, but exports dropped off significantly from 1980 and now appear stabilized at between $15 and $20 million. These figures are official and do not include illicit mining and trade.

In addition to producing and exporting many millions of dollars worth of gems every year, Sri Lanka has also provided the world with some of its most famous and important gemstones. Crown jewels and royal treasuries contain significant sapphires, cat's-eyes, chrysoberyls, and spinels mined over many centuries on Sri Lanka. Most notable of these is probably the British crown jewels, which include the spectacular 104-carat Stuart sapphire, undoubtedly of Sri Lankan origin, and the Black Prince's "ruby," a rounded red spinel weighing approximately 170 carats and of probable Sri Lankan origin. The Queen's jewels also contain the Timur "ruby," a spinel weighing 361 carats. The Smithsonian Institution (National Museum of Natural His-

Figure 1-10. The 138.7-carat Rosser Reeves star ruby from Sri Lanka is considered to be one of the finest in the world. It is part of the gem collection of the National Museum of Natural History (NMNH #G4257). Photo by Dane Penland, courtesy of the Smithsonian Institution.

tory) has its share of important Sri Lankan gemstones, such as the 138.7-carat Rosser Reeves star ruby, possibly the finest of its kind anywhere (Fig. 1-10); the 58.2-carat Maharani cat's-eye chrysoberyl; and a 65.7-carat alexandrite that is thought to be one of the largest in the world. Sri Lankan blue sapphires are well represented at the Smithsonian by the very fine 98.6-carat Bismark and the 423-carat Logan sapphires (Fig. 1-11). The American Museum of Natural History in New York is the repository for one of the finest Padparadscha sapphires, weighing about 100 carats, and the famous Star of India from Sri Lanka. The Natural History Museum of Los Angeles County has some of Sri Lanka's more unusual gemstones in record sizes, most notably a 158-carat sinhalite and a 569-carat phenakite. The state collection in Colombo, Sri Lanka, has a major 362-carat star sapphire, the Star of Sri Lanka. Very fine rough crystals may be as rare or rarer than their faceted counterparts and are highly sought after by museums and individual collectors (Fig. 1-12).

Figure 1-11. The 423-carat Logan sapphire is one of the highlights of the gem collection of the Smithsonian Institution. Photo by Harold and Erica Van Pelt.

Figure 1-12. Often rarer than a well-cut gem is a well-formed crystal of the same material. Crystals such as this beautiful pair of blue sapphires, the larger of which is 3.5 centimeters high, are occasionally found in the gem gravels of Sri Lanka. Photo by Harold and Erica Van Pelt.

REFERENCES

Adams, F. D. 1929. The geology of Ceylon. *Can. Jour. Res.,* 1:425–511.

Bancroft, P. 1984. *Gem and Crystal Treasures.* Western Enterprises–Mineralogical Record, Fallbrook, Cal. 488 pages.

Coates, J. S. 1935. The geology of Ceylon. *Ceylon Jour. Sci.* 19:(B)101–187.

Coomaraswamy, A. K. 1903. Occurrence of corundum in situ near Kandy, Ceylon. *Geol. Mag.* 59:348–350.

Cooray, P.G. 1967. *An Introduction to the Geology of Ceylon.* National Museums of Ceylon, Colombo.

Cooray, P. G., and P. S. Kumarapeli. 1960. Corundum in biotite sillimanite gneiss from near Polgahawela, Ceylon. *Geol. Mag.* 97:480–487.

Dahanayake, K. 1980. Modes of occurrence and provenance of gemstones of Sri Lanka. *Mineralium Deposita* 15:81–86.

Dahanayake, K., A. L. Liyanage, and A. P. Ranasinghe. 1980. Genesis of sedimentary gem deposits in Sri Lanka. *Sedimentary Geology* 25:105–115.

Dissanayake, C. B. 1981. The mineral potential of Sri Lanka, prospects for the future. *Indian Geology Assoc. Bull.* 13(1):23–36.

Fernando, L. J. D. 1948. The geology and mineral deposits of Ceylon. *Bull. Imperial Institute* 46:303–325.

Gübelin, E. 1968. *Die Edelsteine der Insel Ceylon.* Edition Scriptar, S. A., Lausanne. 152 pages.

Guilbert, J. M., and C. F. Park, Jr. 1986. *The Geology of Ore Deposits.* W. H. Freeman and Co., New York. 985 pages.

Gunaratne, H. S. 1976. On the occurrence of gem corundum in Kolonne. *Jour. of Gemmology* 15(1):29–30.

Gunawardene, M., and M. S. Rupasinghe. 1986. The Elahera gem field in central Sri Lanka. *Gems & Gemology* 22:80–95.

Hapuarachchi, D. J. A. C. 1968. Cordierite and wollastonite-bearing rocks of Southwest Ceylon. *Geol. Mag.* 105:317–324.

Herath, J. W. 1982. Mineral resources of Sri Lanka. *Sri Lanka Geol. Surv. Dept. Econ. Bull.* 2.

Katz, M. B. 1969. Cordierite gneisses: Source rock for some gem deposits of Ceylon. *Proc. Ceylon Assoc. Adv. Sci.* 1(abstr.):60–61.

Katz, M. B. 1971. The Precambrian metamorphic rocks of Ceylon. *Geol. Rundschau* 60(4):1523–1549.

Katz, M. B. 1972. On the origin of the Ratnapura-type gem deposits of Ceylon. *Econ. Geol.* 67:113–115.

Keller, P. C. 1983. The rubies of Burma: A review of the Mogok stone tract. *Gems & Gemology* 19(4):209–219.

Lacroix, A. 1891. Gneissose rocks of Salem and Ceylon. *Geol. Surv. India* 24:157–200.

Munasinghe, T., and C. B. Dissanayake. 1981. The origin of gemstones of Sri Lanka. *Econ. Geol.* 76(5):1216–1225.

Perera, N. M. 1939. *Report of the Sub-committee of the Executive Committee of Labor, Industry and Commerce on the Marketing and Cutting of Ceylon Gems.* Ceylon Government Press, Colombo. 34 pages.

Proctor, K. 1984. Gem pegmatites of Minas Gerais, Brazil: Exploration, occurrence, and aquamarine deposits. *Gems & Gemology* 20(2):78–100.

Scalisi, P., and D. Cook. 1983. *Classic Mineral Localities of the World: Asia and Australia.* Van Nostrand Reinhold, New York. 226 pages.

Silva, K. K. M. W. 1976. Some geological aspects of the Elahera gem field, Sri Lanka. 32d Ann. Sessions Sri Lanka Assoc. for the Advancement of Science.

Spencer, L. K., S. D. Dikinis, P. C. Keller, and R. E. Kane. 1988. The diamond deposits of Kalimantan, Borneo. *Gems & Gemology* 24(2):67–80.

Wadia, D. N. and L. J. D. Fernando. 1945. Gems and semiprecious stones of Ceylon. *Ceylon Dept. Mineral Rec. Prof. Pap.* 2:13–44.

Webster, R. 1961. Corundum in Tanganyika. *Gems & Gemology* 10(7):202–205.

Webster, R. 1975. *Gems: Their Sources, Descriptions, and Identification.* 3d ed. Butterworths, London, England.

Wilson, N. W. 1948. The world's diamond deposits. *Mining Mag.* 79:329–341.

Wells, A. J. 1956. Corundum from Ceylon. *Geol. Mag.* 93:25–31.

Zwaan, P. 1974. Garnet, corundum, and other gem minerals from Umba, Tanzania. *Scripta Geol.* 20:41.

Zwaan, P. 1982. Sri Lanka: The gem island. *Gems & Gemology* 18(2):62–71.

2

Gemstones Formed from Surface Water:
The Opals of Australia

Water at or near the earth's surface plays an important role in the formation of some gem minerals. Surface water is capable of dissolving many minerals, particularly when provided a great deal of time to do so. As a result, it carries away components in solution that remain dissolved until, under appropriate conditions, new minerals are deposited. Precious opal and other gemstones form from surface water under special conditions that may include chemical reactions, cooling of waters previously heated by nearby molten rock, and evaporation. Rainwater, for example, combines with atmospheric carbon dioxide to produce carbonic acid, a weak natural acid. If such water seeps into the earth and encounters sulfides (such as pyrite, FeS_2), sulfuric acid, a much stronger acid, is produced, which dissolves minerals, transports their chemical elements, and permeates other rocks to form new minerals.

Among reaction-type minerals formed in this way is malachite—$Cu_2CO_3(OH)_2$—which forms when acidic copper-bearing solutions react with limestone—$CaCO_3$—or dolomite—$CaMg(CO_3)_2$ (Fig. 2-1). Malachite, which is used in jewelry and carvings, usually forms as stalactites and stalagmites in large, open cavities. The world's finest malachite historically comes from the Ural Mountains of the Soviet Union, principally from the Gumeschevsk mine, near Sysert, and the Mednoroudiansk mine in the Nijni Tagil district. Masses of fine malachite weighing up to 250 tons have been recovered from these mines (Scalisi and Cook, 1983). These mines are largely defunct, however, and almost all fine malachite produced today comes from the Katanga district of Zaire.

Rhodochrosite ($MnCO_3$) forms in exactly the same manner as malachite if manganese is present rather than copper. The vividly colored stalactites

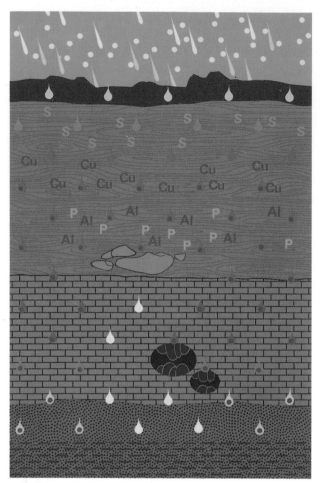

Figure 2-1. Diagram showing the idealized formation process for malachite. Courtesy of the Natural History Museum of Los Angeles County.

Figure 2-2. Diagram showing the idealized process for the formation of amethyst at or near surface temperatures. Courtesy of the Natural History Museum of Los Angeles County.

and stalagmites are beautiful ornamental material. The only commercially important source of such massive rhodochrosite is in Catamarca Province in Argentina, where it occurs interbanded with other carbonates formed at low temperatures.

Turquoise—$CuA1_6(PO_4)_4(OH)_8.4H_2O$—forms in a similar manner where acidic copper-bearing solutions seep into porous volcanic rocks and react with minerals containing aluminum and phosphorus. The rounded, bumpy surfaces on turquoise boulders are typical of minerals that form from cool water. The world's finest turquoise has formed in this manner and historically has come from the Nishapur district of Iran (Gübelin, 1966). Today, very similar material is mined in Hubai Province, China, and vast quantities of turquoise have been produced in the southwestern United States (Pogue, 1919).

Groundwater heated by buried magma, or hydrothermal water, rises toward the surface and dis-

solves chemical elements from the rocks through which it passes. The water cools as it nears the surface, until it can no longer hold the elements in solution. After depositing new minerals, the cooled water sinks back into the earth to be heated again and recycled.

Agate and amethyst (SiO_2) may be formed hydrothermally (Fig. 2-2). If the amount of dissolved silica is great, agate (a form of microcrystalline quartz) is deposited in layers on the walls of cavities in rock. As the silica content of the mineralizing water decreases, large quartz crystals such as amethyst grow on the agate layers until the water is either evaporated or depleted of silica.

Amethyst can be formed over a wide range of temperatures and is, in fact, a relatively common constituent of hydrothermal veins. Lack of geochemical data on these localities prevents definite classification as low-temperature or hydrothermal formations, and for this reason amethyst deposits are described in both types of environment. Some deposits may grade from hydrothermal to the low-temperature (below 50°C) deposits referred to here. Currently, the most important amethyst deposits are in the Artigas district of Uruguay and adjacent Rio Grande do Sul area of Brazil, where amethyst forms the lining of huge cavities in basalt trap rock. Other important Brazilian amethyst deposits are found near Maraba in the state of Pará, where the amethyst fills fractures and cavities in quartzite, and near Pau D'Arco, where the amethyst is thought to be the alluvial equivalent of the Maraba material because it occurs in the same mountain range (Epstein, 1988). Important amethyst deposits are also found in Namazambwe, Zambia, and the Ural Mountains of the Soviet Union.

In arid regions, where rainfall is limited to seasonal showers, the conditions are ideal for the formation of opal deposits by evaporation. During isolated showers, rainwater percolates down through permeable rocks rich in silica (silicon dioxide) such as certain kinds of sediments, volcanic ash, or tuff. Water dissolves silica from these rocks and carries it down to the water table, where it is concentrated. The water table is high during the rainy season, and the water fills open spaces formed by fractures, decomposed organic matter, or dissolved minerals. During the dry season, some of the water evaporates, making the remainder rich in colloidal silica. Finally, opal, a form of solid silica containing water, is deposited in the open spaces in the rock (Fig. 2-3).

Opal consists of billions of submicroscopic spherical particles of silica stacked regularly together. The play of color that characterizes precious opal results from the interplay of light

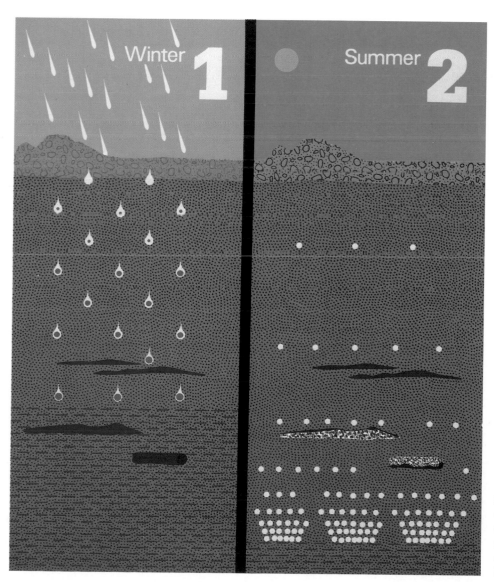

Figure 2-3. Diagram showing the formation of opal with a fluctuating water table. Courtesy of the Natural History Museum of Los Angeles County.

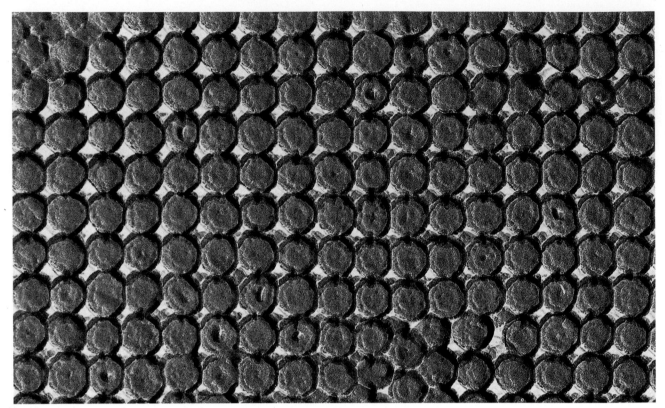

Figure 2-4. *Photomicrograph of precious opal showing orderly arrangement of silica spheres at 50,000 times magnification. Photo by J. V. Sanders.*

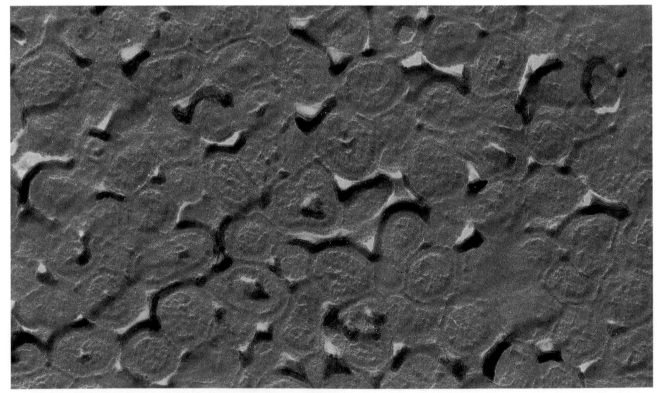

Figure 2-5. *Photomicrograph of common opal showing disordered arrangement of silica spheres at 50,000 times power magnification. Photo by J. V. Sanders.*

(diffraction) with the stacked particles and can occur only when the silica particles are all spheres of the same size that have settled in a very orderly pattern like neat rows of oranges in a box (Fig. 2-4). Most opal is made up of variable-size particles in a disorderly array, and this "potch" opal does not show play of color (Fig. 2-5).

Known opal occurrences are widespread around the world. Geologically, these occurrences can be divided into volcanic and sedimentary, based on their enclosing rock type. Deposits found in volcanic rocks, usually rhyolitic lavas, are generally of high quality but almost invariably contain opal that is too unstable to be suitable for jewelry. Excellent examples of this type of opal are found in Virgin Valley, Nye County, Nevada; Querétaro, Mexico; Dubnik, Czechoslovakia; Gracias, Honduras; and in Indonesia. Typically, these opals occur as vesicle and fracture fillings in the lava. Opals in sedimentary rock are much more stable and therefore are resistant to drying out and cracking. Almost all such opals are found in Australia.

AUSTRALIAN OPAL DEPOSITS

The finest precious opal in the world is mined in the arid, desolate regions of eastern and central Australia. Best known of the deposits are those at Andamooka, Coober Pedy, and Mintabie in South Australia; Lightning Ridge and White Cliffs in New South Wales; and the many smaller deposits in Queensland.

History

The first discovery of opal in Australia is uncertain, but credit is commonly given to Johannes Menge, a German geologist who found opal near Angaston, about 65 km north of Adelaide in South Australia in 1849. However, a recent visit to this area by Ralph Segnit and John Jones (personal communication) revealed only common opal to be present. The first recorded discovery of precious opal in Australia was in 1872, when boulder opal was discovered at Listowel Downs in central Queensland. Sporadic mining took place on a limited basis in the Eromanga mineral field from 1875 to about 1900, and in 1890 the discovery of the White Cliffs opal field, approximately 200 km northeast of Broken Hill in New South Wales, made opal mining a significant industry in Australia. This deposit produced significant quantities of fine opal for 25 years. In 1903 black opal was discovered at Lightning Ridge in northern New South Wales. This new and totally different type of opal with a dark color can at its best show fiery reds and all colors. In 1915, when White Cliffs was in decline, the Coober Pedy opal field in the Stuart Range in South Australia, about 900 km north of Adelaide, was found: It produced huge quantities of opal that was very similar to that found at White Cliffs. The Coober Pedy deposit remains one of the principal producers of opal in Australia today (Kalokerinos, 1971). In 1930, the Andamooka opal field was discovered approximately 600 km north of Adelaide. Although its opal was of a very high quality, today it produces on only a limited scale. The Mintabie deposit is located in a most inhospitable area approximately 240 km northwest of Coober Pedy. Although it had been known for some time, its location deterred significant production until 1976. Today it rivals Coober Pedy as the greatest producer of opal in Australia (Scalisi and Cook, 1983).

General Geology and Occurrence of Opal

Except for the deposit at Mintabie, all significant opal deposits in Australia are confined to Cretaceous marine sediments that were deposited in an area known today as the Great Artesian Basin (Fig. 2-6). During Jurassic and Cretaceous times, the Great Artesian Basin was a shallow inland sea, into which were deposited great thicknesses of sands and sandy clays. These sediments are widespread over portions of New South Wales, Queensland, and parts of South Australia. David (1950) assigned all these opal-bearing units to the Lower Roma series. Subsequent workers have assigned individual unit names for opal-bearing units in each of the opal-producing areas.

The Roma series is typically composed of light bluish gray shales or shaley mudstones with isolated beds of sandstones and limestones. The units above the opal-producing beds are made of leached, soft quartz and kaolin-rich sediments (David, 1950). Capping this is a siliceous duricrust (silcrete), which is highly resistant to weathering and erosional processes (Markham and Basden, 1975).

During the late Cretaceous and early Tertiary periods, the region experienced rapid climatic change: The temperate shallow marine sea became a desert habitat. The Miocene period was a time of regional peneplanation (David, 1950), resulting in a period of deep chemical weathering about 15 to 30 million years ago. This weathering was essential to the formation of opal. The erosional breakdown of feldspars on the surface liberated silica and kaolinitic clays, and the silica was removed in solution by colloidal transport (Markham and Basden, 1975).

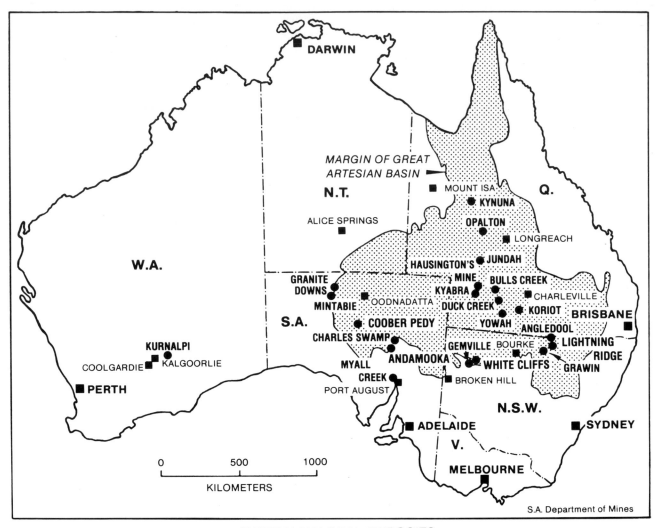

AUSTRALIAN OPAL DEPOSITS

Figure 2-6. Location map showing distribution of major opal deposits in Australia. Courtesy of the Department of Mines and Energy, South Australia.

The water transporting the silica is estimated to be capable of dissolving up to 100 ppm of silica at 20° to 25°C (Darragh et al., 1966). The solution percolated downward to the now lowered ground water table (Jones et al., 1966). This silica-rich solution became trapped in cavities, planar discontinuities, and impermeable layers and replaced wood, shell, and bone (Markham and Basden, 1975), all at shallow levels (Darragh et al., 1966). As the solution remained in its trap, it became increasingly rich in silica by evaporational processes that took place with the general lowering of an otherwise fluctuating water table. When the percentage of silica in solution reached a critical point, the silica developed as minute colloidal particles that agglomerated to form small spheres, creating a gelatinous semisolid. The longer the spheres remained suspended in the soil before the gel formed, the larger the spheres became before settling to the bottom of the trap and forming a layer of uniformly accreted particles. With further evaporation and water absorption from the underlying clays, this mass solidified to form precious opal (Darragh et al., 1966; Jones and Segnit, 1966). Opal forms through the evaporation of silica-rich water. If the water evaporates at a constant rate, solid silica spheres of the same size and shape form. These spheres settle into an orderly array, trapping water between them. The orderly arrangement of silica spheres diffracts light to yield the play of color characteristic of precious opal (Sanders, 1964, 1968). If the water evaporates at an uneven rate, solid silica particles of various shapes and sizes might form. These larger irregular particles settle in a disorderly array and become potch opal, which cannot diffract light or display play of color.

Opal Occurrences

Today these sedimentary host rocks appear as erosional highs at elevations 15 to 20 meters above the recent alluvium that blankets the opal-producing areas (Markham and Basden, 1975). The average depth from the surface to the opal-producing layers is 15 to 25 meters, depending on the topography (Fig. 2-7). Because of the arid environment, the opals in local surface outcrops of opal veins have become desiccated, highly fractured, and economically worthless from their exposure to air (Croll, 1950). In the late 1800s, outcrops of the highly weathered opals led miners to the deposits of fresh opal underground.

White Cliffs, New South Wales

The tiny township of White Cliffs in New South Wales is located about 200 km northeast of Broken Hill. It was officially opened in 1889 and proclaimed the first opal mine in Australia. It has been particularly famous for its crystal opal, a transparent colorless opal displaying an intense play of color. Mining activity waned in 1902, and little activity other than prospecting has taken place at White Cliffs since 1915. The geology at White Cliffs is very similar to that at Lightning Ridge. Opal occurs in horizontal and vertical veins in a claystone. Specimens exhibiting banding of worthless potch and precious opal were common at White Cliffs. Precious opal also commonly replaced fossil shell and wood and is best known among collectors for its opal pseudomorphs after glauberite (Gurich,

1901). The most spectacular opal replacement found was a complete skeleton of a plesiosaur-like animal, almost all of precious opal.

The sequence of sediments from the surface downward is described for this area as follows (Ralph, 1961):

1. A siliceous material, Grey Billy. It has a maximum thickness of 20 feet.
2. A layer of clays with small clasts of Grey Billy incorporated within the beds. The maximum thickness is about 11 feet, but in some areas it is totally absent.
3. A siliceous unit created of pisoliths similar to Grey Billy that is believed to represent an older paleo surface level. Commonly known as *geyser*, it has a maximum thickness of 8 feet.
4. A thinly bedded unit of fine-grained sandstones with a clayey matrix. The parent material is believed to be feldspathic sandstones.
5. *Bandstone* is fine-grained sandstone that has had high-silica secondary fluids pass through and solidify. Just below this level is where most of the profitable mining takes place.

The opal occurs in this area as thick veinlets within the host material. It is discontinuous laterally. Many of the fossils, including wood pieces, have been replaced by opal (MacNevin and Holmes, 1977). Because of the massive mining activity around White Cliffs in the earlier part of this century, most of the area has been worked out (Croll, 1950). In the mid-1980s, however, mining activity has been renewed with the introduction of heavy equipment.

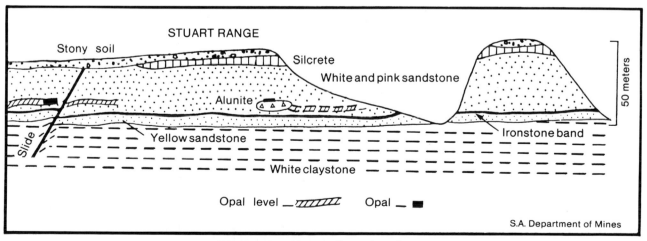

Diagrammatic section showing
OPAL OCCURRENCE at COOBER PEDY

Figure 2-7. Idealized geological cross-section of opal beds at Coober Pedy. Courtesy of the Department of Mines and Energy, South Australia.

Lightning Ridge, New South Wales

Lightning Ridge is located in central northern New South Wales, about 770 km from Sydney. It has produced the finest opals in the world since it was first mined commercially in 1901 (MacNevin and Holmes, 1977). Lightning Ridge is most famous for its black opals (Figs. 2-8 and 2-9), which have red, blue, and yellow fire with a dark rather than white matrix; pure black potch is also found here. The opal typically is found as irregular nodules, or "nobbies," that may represent the opal replacement of sponges or corals. It also occurs as thin seams in vertical and horizontal joints in a characteristically soft gray Finch Claystone that turns white and hardens upon drying. The Finch Claystone, or "opal dirt," is 1 to 6 meters thick and may be as much as 30 meters below the surface. It is Cretaceous in age, as are all the sediments at Lightning Ridge. Opal commonly occurs near the junction of the Finch Claystone and the overlying Wallangulla Sandstone. This overlying unit is 2 to 10 meters thick with a very hard silicified base called the *steel band.* Capping the Cretaceous sequence is a fine-grained white Coocoran Claystone up to 4 meters thick that is nicknamed "shin cracker" because it hardens when exposed at the surface. Most of the opal is found 6 to 10 meters below the surface (Whiting and Ralph, 1961).

Figure 2-8. *The striking play of color against a dark background is characteristic of black opal from Lightning Ridge, New South Wales. Photo by Harold and Erica Van Pelt.*

Figure 2-9. *This 26-carat opal from the J. Traurig collection is a spectacular example of fine black opal from Lightning Ridge, New South Wales, Australia. Photo by Harold and Erica Van Pelt.*

Coober Pedy, South Australia

The Coober Pedy mining area is in the Stuart Range of South Australia about 970 km north of Adelaide (Fig. 2-10). It opened in 1915 but did not see massive expansion until 1919, when the value of opals suddenly tripled because of the postwar demand. Today, Coober Pedy is the largest producer of opals in Australia. The opal workings extend for almost 40 km along the range. The name *Coober Pedy (Kupapiti)* is the aboriginal term for "white man in a hole" (Hiern, 1965); the miners here lived below ground because such housing was cheap to excavate and enabled them to escape the heat and flies during the extreme summer heat. The most comprehensive description of Coober Pedy has been written by Barnes and Townsend (1982). Other important references include Hiern (1967), Winton (1925), and Jones and Segnit (1966).

The ground surface at Coober Pedy is covered by *gibbers*, siliceous boulders (silcrete) that range in diameter from 1 to 25 centimeters. These boulders form an almost continuous layer over the topography and at places can make walking difficult.

Opal occurs in layers up to 30 meters below the surface. Immediately below the surface is a siliceous crust about 2 meters thick that is so resistant to erosion that it commonly has created low tabletop mesas in the surrounding area. Immediately below the siliceous crust is a highly weathered pink claystone approximately 10 to 15 meters thick, with another siliceous layer at its base. Most opal is found in the next layer, which is pink to brown sandstone with veins of precious opal running through it. Opal pseudomorphs after shell are common (Fig. 2-11). The main opal layer is about 30 meters below the surface (Keeling, 1977). Mining operations at Coober Pedy are typical of those

Figure 2-10. Overview from the east of opal deposit at Coober Pedy in South Australia. Photo courtesy of the Department of Mines and Energy, South Australia.

Figure 2-11. *Opalized clam shells from Coober Pedy, South Australia. Specimen measures approximately 10.5 by 7.5 cm. Photo by Harold and Erica Van Pelt.*

Figure 2-12. In the opal fields of Coober Pedy, South Australia, large drilling rigs or blowers bore cylindrical shafts down to the opal-bearing strata. Photo courtesy of the Department of Mines and Energy, South Australia.

Figure 2-13. Tunneling machine working underground at Coober Pedy, South Australia. Photo courtesy of the Department of Mines and Energy, South Australia.

Figure 2-14. Large drilling rig working at Coober Pedy, South Australia. Photo courtesy of the Department of Mines and Energy, South Australia.

found elsewhere in Australia, using blowers (Fig. 2-12), tunneling machines (Fig. 2-13), and large drilling rigs (Fig. 2-14).

Andamooka, South Australia

Andamooka is just west of Lake Torrens, 600 km north of Adelaide, and near the great Olympic Dam copper-silver-uranium deposit. It was discovered in 1930 by two boundary riders who found surface fragments of opal below what is now Treloar Hill. The first commercial mining began in 1933. Mining today extends over a 13-km by 5-km area. An excellent description of Andamooka can be found in Barnes and Townsend (1982).

The sedimentary sequence at Andamooka is almost identical to Coober Pedy (Johns, 1968). The opal is found approximately 25 meters below the surface at the junctions of the underlying clay and overlying sandstone beds. It fills cracks and cavities in a thin band about 30 cm thick that miners termed *concrete band conglomerate*. Below the opal-producing bed are 8 to 10 meters of Jurassic Algebuckina sandstone, which lies unconformably over Upper Precambrian Tent Hill Formation quartzite. A detailed discussion of the geology can be found in Nixon (1960). The living facilities at Andamooka, like those at Coober Pedy, are rather spartan. The supply of water drawn from surrounding wells is just enough to supply people's drinking needs, and in dry periods water must be brought by tanker from nearby artesian wells. Because the mines are near larger towns and the roads to the area are good, buyers from Sydney and other cities can drive right to the township and negotiate directly with the miners (Croll, 1950). However, Andamooka has steadily declined in production since the early 1970s, and many miners have given up their claims in favor of the Coober Pedy or Mintabie areas.

Mintabie, South Australia

The Mintabie opal field, located about 240 km northwest of Coober Pedy, is second only to that area in its production of fine opal. The Mintabie deposit is particularly significant because it produces some black opal that rivals the finest from the classic Lightning Ridge source. The deposit was first discovered in 1921 during the digging of a water well (Barnes and Townsend, 1982), but, due to its remoteness and lack of water, it was not worked commercially until 1976. Mining activity mushroomed with the discovery of a major deposit of fine opal in 1977 and remains high today. Detailed descriptions of Mintabie are found in Hiern

(1967) and particularly in Barnes and Townsend (1982).

According to Townsend (1981), the geology of the Mintabie deposit is not like any other opal deposit in Australia, in that the opal occurs in Paleozoic rather than Cretaceous rocks. The Mintabie beds are a series of gently dipping kaolinitic white sandstones whose age has been determined by the early Cretaceous claystones and clayey sands above them. They are possibly Devonian.

The Mintabie beds exhibit widespread surface exposures. Opal is found in the upper parts of the beds, where they exhibit pronounced vertical and oblique jointing, and in less silicified sandstones down to depths of 20 meters. The beds also exhibit cross-bedding, and opal seams develop along these cross-bedding structures.

Mining at Mintabie has been almost exclusively open pit with the aid of bulldozers, trench diggers, and blasting. Today, however, underground mining is gradually replacing the open pit operations. Opal has been found as far as 8 km away, and the potential of Mintabie is great.

Queensland

Queensland opal occurrences are widespread in a 300-km-wide belt extending from near Hungerford on the border with New South Wales northwest 900 km to the Winton area. The most prolific mining areas are the Eromanga and Quilpie districts in the south and Winton and Opalton in the north. According to Senior and associates (1977), who wrote a comprehensive report of the geology of Queensland's opal deposits, known opal deposits in that state number about 60.

The opal deposits of southwestern Queensland have been worked since about 1875, when, according to Connah (1966), activity was concentrated in the Eromanga mineral field. Production into the twentieth century was sporadic, at best, due to the inhospitable terrain. Jackson (1902) wrote that most of the mines were deserted when he visited the area in 1901. With the introduction of open pit mining in the 1960s, the area became active once again, and Senior and associates (1977) reported a peak in mining activity in 1973, when 20 bulldozers were working in the Eromanga area alone. Mining activity has declined since then with the depletion of old workings and the lack of any new discoveries despite the geological potential of the area. The Hayricks mine, located about 80 km northwest of Quilpie, is the only significant producer today.

All of the opal deposits in Queensland are found in the Eromanga Basin, which is part of the much larger Great Artesian Basin of Australia. The opal is confined to the Winton Formation of Late Cretaceous age and, like opals elsewhere in Australia, is a product of deep chemical weathering. In Queensland, the opal is typically associated with kaolinitic weathered areas, and almost all the opal is found within ironstone-enriched layers, lenses, and concretions.

Opal from Queensland is very distinctive. It is characteristically bright blue, green, and red in an ironstone boulder matrix that is typically rounded concretions with desiccation cracks that provided the open spaces necessary for opal deposition. The width of the fracture and the quality of the opal appear to be correlated. The narrower the fracture, the finer the opal. Because much of this boulder opal occurs in thin veins, it is usually cut as a natural doublet with an ironstone backing. Yowah nuts, the small, hollow ironstone concretions found at the Yowah opal field near Eulo Station, are an exception. They are rarely larger than 5 cm in diameter, about walnut size.

Prior to 1958, all opal mining was done by hand. A shaft was sunk to the opal layer (usually about 25 meters), and then the miner used a hand pick to follow the worthless potch opal. On seeing a flash of precious opal, the miner would gently carve the sandy clay away so that no precious opal would be fractured. The opal-rich material was then taken to the surface and run through a puddler, a wood sluice with gratings through which water ran, to remove the clay and sand and leave only the noble opal.

Today miners sink their shafts with the aid of large drill rigs. Tunnels are excavated with horizontal augers or dug out by means of explosives and jackhammers, which are also used to follow signs of opal. The hand pick may still be used to extract good material. The debris is removed by buckets raised by machinery and automatically emptied at the surface, or removed by means of blowers (Fig. 2-12), a kind of large vacuum machine. Bulk material from the opal horizon may be treated by means of wet or dry puddling. Dry puddling (rumbling) is a new technique used only within the last 5 to 10 years. It uses the same principle as the original puddler but it uses no water, which is important in an arid environment. Open pit mining using bulldozers has been employed at most fields, especially Mintabi, where the ground is harder. The top 50 to 60 feet are removed to expose the opal layers, but this method has not proved particularly profitable and is unpopular with the mining community (Holmes et al., 1982).

A profitable technique for the professional and the amateur alike is *noodling*, which is picking through discarded mining material to look for opal. However, the visitor must be careful not to intrude on a claim being worked! Some miners have taken to using large conveyer belts loaded with the opal-rich discarded material and subjecting it to ultraviolet light to detect the opals (Australian Gem Industry Association, 1983), as some opal fluoresces brightly.

Famous Opals

South Australia produces more than 80 percent of the world's opal. Accurate opal production figures prior to 1971 are very difficult to obtain, but conservative estimates for South Australia are approximately $41 million for the period ending in 1971. According to the better records that have been kept since then, South Australia produced $204 million in opal up to 1977, and an average of about $40 million annually since 1977 (Barnes and Townsend, 1982).

An excellent discussion of the famous opals of Australia can be found in Leechman (1961). By far the most spectacular and famous opals are the incredible black opals from Lightning Ridge. The Butterfly or Red Admiral stone from Lightning Ridge is considered to be one of the most beautiful opals in the world. Found in 1922, it weighs about 50 carats.

Other famous Lightning Ridge opals include the Empress, Black Prince, Pride of Australia (226 carats), Crystal Princess, Flame Queen, Pandora (711 carats), and Light of the World (252 carats) (Bancroft, 1984).

Other opal-producing areas have also produced noteworthy gems. One of the largest uncut gem opals was the Noolinga Neera, an 86-ounce mass found about 4 meters below the surface by a group of Australian Aborigines at Andamooka. It was cut into a 205-carat oval stone (Scalisi and Cook, 1983).

The Olympic Australis, weighing almost 20,000 carats, is one of the largest uncut opals in existence. It was found at Coober Pedy in 1956 and named for the Melbourne Olympic Games and the Aurora Australis.

The only opal assigned to royalty is the Andamooka Opal. It weighed 6 ounces when found in 1949 and was cut into a 203-carat cabochon. This stone was set into a necklace and presented to Her Majesty Queen Elizabeth II.

The National Gem Collection in the Smithsonian Institution has numerous important Australian opals, including white opals weighing 345, 162, 155,

146, and 105 carats and black opals weighing 58.8, 54.3, and 44 carats. In 1985 the Smithsonian Institution was presented with the Zale's opal, a 318.44-carat, polished free form from Australia.

REFERENCES

Australian Gem Industry Association. 1983. *Australian Opals and Gemstones: Nature's Own Fireworks.* The Australian Gem Industry Ass'n. Lim., Sydney, pp. 2–11.

Bancroft, P. 1984. *Gem and Crystal Treasures.* Western Enterprises–Mineralogical Record, Fallbrook, CA, 488 pages.

Barnes, L. C., and I. J. Townsend. 1982. *Opal, South Australia's Gemstone.* Geol. Survey of South Australia Handbook 5. D. J. Woolman, Eastwood, S. Australia. 157 pages.

Connah, T. H. 1966. A prospector's guide to opal in western Queensland. *Queensland Government Mining Journal* 67:23–39.

Croll, I. C. H. 1950. Opal industry of Australia. *Bureau of Mineral Resources Geology and Geophysics (Australia) Bull.* 17:7–47.

Darragh, P. J., A. J. Gaskin, B. C. Terrell, and J. V. Sanders. 1966. Origin of precious opal. *Nature* 209:13–16.

David, T. W. E. 1950. *The Geology of the Commonwealth of Australia.* I (of III):482–487.

Epstein, D. 1988. Amethyst mining in Brazil. *Gems & Gemology* 24:214–228.

Gübelin, E. 1966. The ancient turquoise mines in Iran. *Gems & Gemology* 12:3–13.

Gurich, G. 1901. Edelopal und Opal: Pseudomorphosen von White Cliffs, Australia. *Neues Jahrb. Mineralogie* 14:472–483.

Hiern, M. N. 1967. Opal deposits at Coober Pedy. *Q. geol. Notes, Geol. Surv. S. Aust.* 13:6–7.

Hiern, M. N. 1967. Coober Pedy opal field; deposits in northern South Australia; Mintabie opal field; Myall Creek opal field. *Min. Rev. (Adelaide)* 122:5–22.

Holmes, G., S. R. Lishmund, and G. M. Oakes. 1982. A review of industrial minerals and rocks in New South Wales. Geological Survey of New South Wales. *Dept. of Mineral Resources Bull.* 30:199–202.

Jackson, C. F. V. 1902. *The Opal Mining Industry and Distribution of Opal Deposits in Queensland.* Geological Survey of Queensland Publication 177.

Johns, R. K. 1968. Geology and mineral resources of the Andamooka-Torrens area. *Bull. Geol. Surv. S. Aust.* 41:103.

Jones, J. B., J. Biddle, and E. R. Segnit. 1966. Opal genesis. *Nature* 210:1353–1354.

Jones, J. B., and E. R. Segnit. 1966. The occurrence and formation of opal at Coober Pedy and Andamooka. *Aust. Jour. Sci.* 29:129–133.

Kalokerinos, A. 1971. *Australian Precious Opal.* Thomas Nelson (Aust.) Ltd., Melbourne.

Keeling, J. L. 1977. *Opal in South Australia.* Mineral Information Series, Department of Mines and Energy. Eastwood, S. Australia, 16 pages.

Leechman, F. 1961. *The Opal Book.* Ure Smith, Sydney. 263 pages.

MacNevin, A. A. and G. Holmes. 1977. *Mineral Industry of New South Wales No. 18: Gemstones.* 2d ed. New South Wales Geological Survey, Sydney.

Markham, N. C., and H. Basden. 1975. *The Mineral Deposits of New South Wales.* Geological Survey of New South Wales, Department of Mines, Sydney, Australia, 525–533.

Nixon, L. G. B. 1960. Andamooka opal field. *Min. Rev. (Adelaide)* 109:13–23.

Pogue, J. E. 1919. *The Turquois.* 3d memoir, National Academy of Sciences 3.

Ralph, R. E. 1961. *The White Cliffs Opal Field, New South Wales.* New South Wales Department of Mines Technical Report 7 for 1959, Sydney, Australia, 7–18.

Sanders, J. V. 1964. Colour of precious opal. *Nature* 204:1151–1153.

Sanders, J. V. 1968. *Diffraction of Light by Opals.* Acta Crysta 424:427–436.

Scalisi, P., and D. Cook. 1983. *Classic Mineral Localities of the World: Asia and Australia.* Van Nostrand Reinhold, New York. 228 pages.

Senior, B., D. McColl, B. Long, and R. Whiteley. 1977. The geology and magnetic characteristics of precious opal deposits, Southwest Queensland. *Jour. Australian Geol. Geophysics* 2:241–251.

Stone, D. M., and R. A. Butt. 1976. *Australian Precious Opal.* Periwinkle Books, Sydney.

Townsend, I. J. 1981. Discovery of early Cretaceous sediments at Mintabie opal field. *Q. geol. Notes, Geol. Sur. S. Aust.* 77:8–15.

Whiting, J. W., and R. E. Ralph. 1961. *The Occurrence of Opal at Lightning Ridge and Grawin, with Geological Notes on County Finch.* New South Wales Department of Mines Technical Report 6 for 1958, Sydney, Australia, 7–21.

Winton, L. J. 1925. The Coober Pedy (Stuart's Range) opal field. *South Australia Mining Review* 42.

PART II

Gemstones of Igneous-Hydrothermal Origin

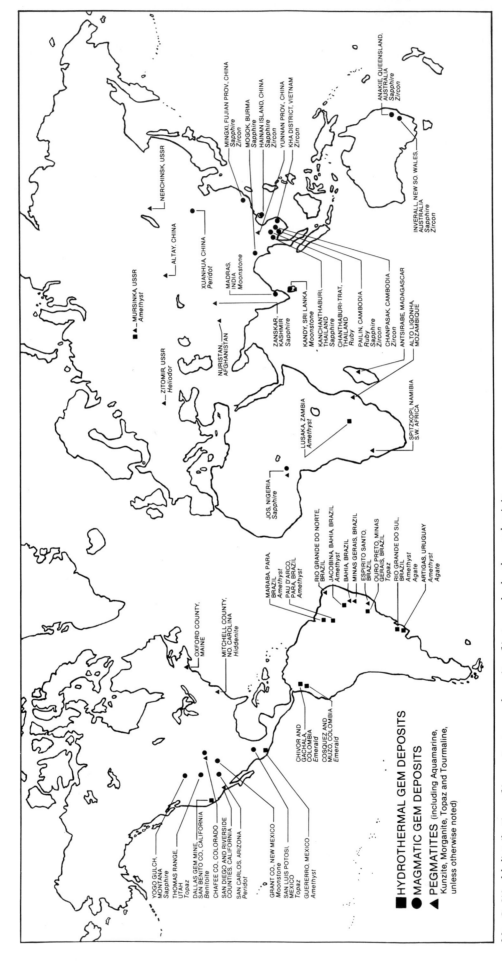

Map 2. *World distribution of important gem deposits of igneous-hydrothermal origin.*

Very hot water vapors escaping from magmas deep in the earth's crust are known as hydrothermal fluids (from hydro, meaning "water," and thermal, meaning "hot"). These fluids often carry rare elements, such as fluorine and beryllium, away from the magma via fractures in surrounding rocks and sometimes combine with near-surface water to pick up additional elements. The resulting solutions eventually cool and form mineral veins in the fractures. Under appropriate physical and chemical conditions, these veins may contain gemstones such as topaz, amethyst, benitoite, and emerald.

Topaz, especially, is found in a variety of environments. The most valuable topaz occurs in hydrothermal veins near Ouro Prêto, Minas Gerais, Brazil. Here, so-called imperial topaz occurs in deeply weathered veins of potassium feldspar and quartz (Keller, 1983; Olsen, 1971). Amethyst is a common component of hydrothermal veins, especially in metallic ore deposits. Benitoite, one of the rarest of gemstones, is found only in hydrothermal veins that cut serpentine bodies in the coast range of San Benito County, California (Louderback, 1907).

The most important of the hydrothermal gemstone deposits is the emerald-mining district at Muzo, Colombia. This deposit in the Andes Mountains of central Colombia, 60 miles north of the capital city of Bogotá, has yielded the finest emeralds in the world for more than 400 years.

Pegmatites, granitelike rocks with very large crystals, produce more kinds of gemstone than any other type of deposit. A pegmatite forms when the water-rich portion of molten granite is squeezed into a fracture in the solid surrounding rock. As the pegmatite liquid cools in the fracture, it begins to solidify at the outer walls first and then toward the center. The liquid changes in composition, and the minerals forming from it also change to create layers (or zones) of minerals. The last fluid remaining in cavities in the center of the pegmatite is very hot water containing rare elements such as beryllium, boron, and lithium. Gemstone crystals may form from this fluid to create gem pockets. Pegmatites are found throughout the world (Sinkankas, 1981). The Pala area of San Diego County, California (Jahns and Wright, 1951), the Sverdlovsk region of the Soviet Urals (Bauer, 1904), and recently the Altai area of northwestern China (Keller and Wang, 1986) and the Nuristan area of Afghanistan are among the most important. No area can match the pegmatite region of Minas Gerais, Brazil, for its sheer volume of production. Since World War II, Brazil, especially Minas Gerais, has eclipsed the rest of the world in the production of pegmatitic gemstones.

Water plays an essential role in the formation of all the deposits considered thus far. Such is not the case for gemstones such as ruby, sapphire, moonstone, and zircon, which grow directly from molten rock while it is still deep in the earth. The magma must cool slowly at first to allow the gemstone crystals to grow. Then, while most of the magma is still liquid, it rushes upward, carrying the gem crystals with it. It cools and solidifies in fractures near the surface or as volcanic lava on the surface. Most often the magma is alkali basalt.

Today, most of the world's peridot comes from mantle-derived inclusions in a single alkali basalt deposit on the San Carlos Indian Reservation in Gila County, Arizona. Alkali basalts are dark volcanic rocks that are the result of the partial melting of rocks in the mantle at depths between 20 and 60 miles. The molten rock rises rapidly and explosively to the earth's surface, where it erupts as a volcano. Often alkali basalts carry with them solid fragments of mantlerock containing abundant forsterite olivine, which sometimes occurs in large, transparent, gem-quality nodules.

37

Alkali basalts, almost always deeply weathered, supply the world with most of its rubies, sapphires, and zircons. These deposits are commonly regionally widespread, such as at Inverell, New South Wales, and Anakie, Queensland, areas in Australia, in Fujian Province, China (Keller and Keller, 1986), and especially in Indochina.

In tropical climates alkali basalts decompose rapidly, leaving the gem crystals behind to accumulate in alluvial gravels. Southeastern Thailand now produces more than 70 percent of the world's fine rubies from decomposing basalts or the resulting alluvial gravels (Keller, 1982) (Map 2).

REFERENCES

Bauer, M., and L. J. Spencer. 1904. *Precious Stones* (trans. of 1896 German text). Charles Griffin & Co., London. 647 pages.

Keller, P. C. 1982. The Chanthaburi-Trat gemfield, Thailand. *Gems & Gemology* 18(4):186–196.

Keller, P. C. 1983. The Capao Topaz deposits, Ouro Prêto, Minas Gerais, Brazil. *Gems & Gemology* 19(1):12–20.

Keller, A. S., and P. C. Keller. 1986. The sapphires of Mingxi, Fujian Prov., China. *Gems & Gemology* 22(1):41–45.

Keller, P. C., and F. Wang. 1986. A survey of the gemstone resources of China. *Gems & Gemology* 22(1):3-13.

Louderback, G. E. 1907. Benitoite, a new California gem mineral. *Bulletin of the Dept. of Geology, Univ. of California* 5(9).

Olsen, D. R. 1971. Origin of topaz deposits near Ouro Prêto, Minas Gerais, Brazil. *Econ. Geol.* 66(4):627–631.

3

Hydrothermal Gem Deposits:
The Emerald Deposits of Colombia

When hot magma rises through the earth's crust, it often fails to reach the surface to erupt as a volcano. Instead, it forms large magma bodies that cool very slowly to form large granitic masses, which, if large enough, are called *batholiths*.

Around the edges of the cooling magma, hot, mineral-rich solutions are given off and mix with cooler circulating groundwaters that percolate downward from the surface. With the heat from the still hot magma as a driving force, the hydrothermal solutions circulate continuously through available fractures and pores in the surrounding rock and constantly leach additional elements from both the cooling magma and the surrounding rock (Fig. 3-1). When temperatures and pressures are high, water is capable of dissolving and transporting large amounts of minerals. If such solution is very basic (high pH), it dissolves and transports much quartz, thus accounting for its abundance as a vein mineral. In time, the solutions, now laden

with a wide array of elements, cool, and minerals crystallize in any existing opening in the surrounding rocks, such as those formed by tension fractures or faults created by the force of the intruding magma, gas cavities in an overlying lava flow, or bedding planes in layered sedimentary rocks. Every type of opening, in every type of rock, is susceptible to hydrothermal invasion.

Hydrothermal deposits, which range in temperature from 50°C to 500°C, form many of our most important precious and base metal deposits and also some of our more interesting gem deposits, including those containing amethyst, topaz, red beryl, benitoite, and the world's finest emerald.

The nature of these powerful mineralizing hydrothermal solutions has been the subject of much speculation. Geochemists have examined three basic lines of evidence to solve the mystery: (1) hot springs, where the mineralizing process can be observed today; (2) fluid inclusions found in crystals,

39

**Gemstones Formed
in Hydrothermal Veins**

Continental crust

Mineral deposits
in veins

Depth in miles

0

½

1

1½

2

Molten rock

*Figure 3-1. Diagram showing process leading to the
formation of hydrothermal gem deposits. Courtesy of the
Natural History Museum of Los Angeles County.*

which represent a direct sample of the mineralizing fluid; and (3) the alteration of rocks surrounding deposits.

The formation of hydrothermal deposits requires mineralizing solutions capable of dissolving

and transporting minerals, openings in the surrounding rocks through which the solutions can
be channeled, sites for the deposition of the minerals, and a chemical reaction, cooling, or drop in
pressure for deposition.

Fissure veins, the most common and important form of hydrothermal deposit, require the formation of the fissure itself and the mineralizing
process to fill that fissure. The two processes may
or may not be separated by a long period of time.
Most fissure veins are narrow and range in length
from a few feet to a few miles. Usually, the fissure
veins are found in groups that form systems.

Although many factors may be involved in hydrothermal deposition, including chemical reactions similar to those responsible for turquoise and
malachite at lower temperatures, the most important factors are changes in temperature and pressure. In general, a drop in temperature and/or
pressure decreases a mineral's solubility and
causes crystallization. Veins commonly change in
mineralogical character with depth because of the
changes in temperature and pressure at the time
of deposition. Vein intersections and increases in
width are common causes for the drop in pressure
that causes mineral deposition.

Hydrothermal solutions start their journey
with heat supplied by the magma, and the solutions naturally cool as they travel away from the
source. The rate of cooling depends on the character of the surrounding rock and the size of the
channel.

Likewise, solutions are usually generated at
great depth under high pressure. As they travel
upward through the crust, pressure lessens and
crystallization takes place.

Many hydrothermal veins consist of solid interlocking grains of various mineral species but may
contain well-formed crystals pointing to the center
of the vein away from the wall rock.

The hydrothermal vein minerals usually reflect
the type of rock the fluids have flowed through and
the type of magma that gave rise to the fluids initially. Quartz is by far the most common vein mineral in hydrothermal deposits, and feldspar is also
common. If the fluids passed through calcium-rich
sediments, such as in the case of the Colombian
emerald deposits, however, the major vein mineral
may be calcite.

Hydrothermal gem deposits are widespread
around the world. The most common are amethyst
deposits, such as those of the Ural Mountains in
the Soviet Union and in Mexico, Zambia, and Brazil.

The world's finest amethyst comes from hydrothermal veins in the 75 amethyst localities in
the Mursinka district in the Soviet Urals, Tusha-

kalva being the most important. Here, amethyst occurs with drusy quartz in veins that cross a weathered granite (Scalisi and Cook, 1983). Similar deposits are found near Maraba and Pau d'Arco, both in Pará, and in Rio Grande do Sul, Brazil. Amethyst is also commercially mined in Guererro, Mexico; Lusaka, Zambia; and Artigas, Uruguay. Some of these have been noted in Chapter 2 for lower temperature deposits.

Many of the world's topaz deposits are of pegmatitic origin. However, a unique and highly desirable variety, aptly called *Imperial*, comes from highly weathered hydrothermal veins in the area of Ouro Prêto, in Minas Gerais, Brazil (Keller, 1983). Topaz euclase, muscovite quartz, and hematite were deposited with large amounts of orthoclase as hydrothermal fluids filled tension fractures in the Sabara formation, a phyllite of Precambrian age. Deep chemical weathering has reduced the phyllite to clay and the orthoclase to kaolin, leaving the resistant topaz, enclase, hematite, and quartz (Olsen, 1971).

Benitoite, the beautiful and rare state gemstone of California, is found only in hydrothermal veins cutting serpentinous rocks near the headwaters of the San Benito River in San Benito County, California. These veins, up to 5 cm thick, consist almost entirely of fibrous white natrolite. The benitoite crystals occur with black neptunite and dark red joaquinite and are usually attached to the serpentine vein wall (Louderback, 1907).

By far the most important hydrothermal gem deposits are the emerald deposits of Colombia. These deposits are unique in that most of the world's emeralds occur in metamorphic rocks as a by-product of that environment. Recently, emeralds have been reported in hydrothermal veins from Panjahir, Afghanistan (Bowersox, 1985). In Colombia, however, calcite-rich hydrothermal veins crossing Cretaceous sediments yield the world's finest emeralds.

COLOMBIAN EMERALD DEPOSITS

The two principal emerald-mining districts in Colombia today are Muzo and Chivor. The 360-square-km Muzo district, at an elevation of about 600 m, is located 105 km north of the capital city of Bogotá in the valley of the Río Itoco, a tributary of the Río Minero. The main mines in the Muzo district include the Tequendama, Santa Barbara, El Chulo, Coscucz, and Peñas Blancas (Fig. 3-2). The district is owned by the Colombian government

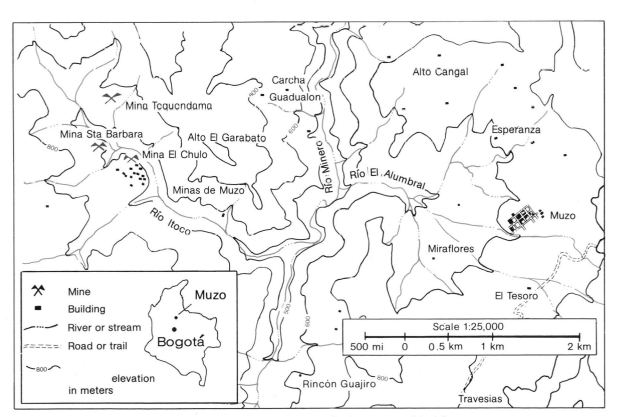

Figure 3-2. Index map showing the location of the mines and other geographical features of the Muzo district, Boyacá, Colombia.

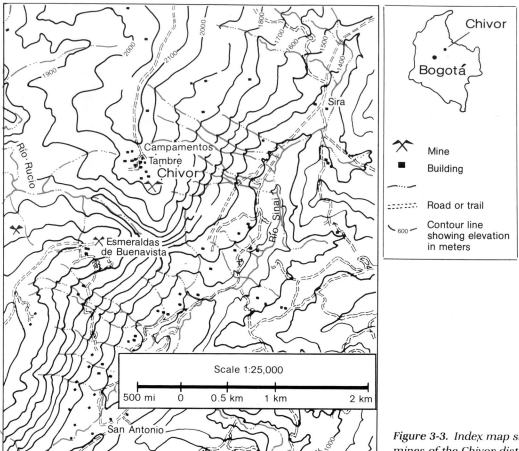

Figure 3-3. Index map showing location of mines of the Chivor district, Almeida, Boyacá, Colombia.

and is currently being worked by several private mining companies operating under restricted leases.

The Chivor district, located about 75 km northeast of Bogotá in the Almeida township of Boyacá, is part of the exceedingly rugged country where the Río Rucio and Río Sinai join to form the Río Guavio (Fig. 3-3). Feininger (1970) points out that the mine is at an elevation of about 2,300 m and that just 2 km to the east, in sight of the mine, the Río Guavio, at an elevation of only 700 m, slices through a ridge that is even higher than the mine. In addition to the Chivor mine, the Chivor district includes the Buenavista mine, immediately to the south of Chivor, and the Las Vegas de San Juan mine, located 8 km to the southwest and commonly known as the Gachalá mine (Anderton, 1955). The Chivor mine is the only major privately owned emerald mine in Colombia. The Buenavista and Gachalá mines operate as concessions under a 1959 law, and their owners pay a 25 percent royalty to the Colombian government (Colombian American Business, 1979).

Over the past half century, numerous papers have described the Colombian emerald mines, usually from the view of recent visitors to the mining areas (MacFadden, 1934; Switzer, 1948; Copeland, 1950; Anderton, 1950, 1965; Bancroft, 1971; Tenhagen, 1972; Ringsrud, 1986). A detailed overview of the Colombia deposits is found in Keller (1981); see Sinkankas (1981) for additional references.

History

Emeralds mined in Colombia have been used for trade and personal adornment throughout much of Central and South America since pre-Columbian times (Bray, 1978; Dominguez, 1965). When the first Spaniards arrived in the New World in the early sixteenth century, emeralds were being traded as far south as Peru and Chile and as far north as Mexico. Reportedly, the Spanish conqueror Pizarro sent four chests of emeralds, undoubtedly of Colombian origin, from Peru to the king of Spain in 1533 (Ball, 1931). Possibly the famous Inquisition necklace is an example of such emeralds (Fig. 3-4).

Figure 3-4. *The 300-year-old Spanish Inquisition necklace contains 15 emerald beads and more than 360 diamonds. It is part of the gem collection of the National Museum of Natural History, Washington, D.C. (NMNH #G5113). Photo by Harold and Erica Van Pelt.*

Figure 3-5. A view looking east over the Chivor emerald mine, which is situated at an elevation of about 2,300 m. Photo by Peter C. Keller.

Chivor was the first operating emerald mine discovered by the Spaniards in their conquest of the New World (Klein, 1941) (Fig. 3-5). Gonzalo Jimenez de Quesada saw the first sign of emeralds in Colombia at Turqmeque, Boyacá, in 1537 (Colombian American Business, 1979). Quesada sent Captain Pedro F. de Valenzuela to find the source. That same year, he located the well-developed Chibcha Indian mine of Somondoco, later to be named Chivor after a nearby valley. Soon thereafter, the Spaniards were vigorously working the Chivor mine with local Indians as slave labor.

Five years after the founding of Santisima Trinidad de los Muzos in 1559 (Wokittel, 1960), the Muzo and Caijma Indians' mine was located some 7 km to the west on the Itoco Hill. The Spaniards began mining the Muzo area in 1567, and initial production is said to have overshadowed production at Chivor (Feininger, 1970). By the end of the sixteenth century, both Chivor and Muzo were vigorously worked by Indian slave labor. In 1592, the first recorded grant of Chivor was given to Francisco Maldonado de Mendoza by Antonio Gonzalez, president of the New Kingdom of Granada. By this time, however, the treatment of the Indian slaves was so inhumane that on September 22, 1593, President Gonzalez issued a 39-article decree protecting the Indians (Johnson, 1961). This decree was soon followed in 1602 by several royal orders

from Phillip III of Spain to enforce the law. By this time, however, the Indian population had already been decimated. As a consequence of this loss of cheap labor and the litigation that followed the royal orders, production of Colombian emeralds declined drastically. In 1650, the Muzo mines were declared royal property, and production further declined. By 1675, the Chivor mine had been abandoned; its location became a mystery that endured for over 200 years. Muzo continued to be worked sporadically throughout the seventeenth, eighteenth, and nineteenth centuries (Barriga and Barriga, 1973) until the government declared it the National Emerald Domain in 1871 (Colombian American Business, 1979). When the mines at Muzo came under government control, production all but ceased, and lawless disorder came to characterize the area. This situation has changed only very recently.

Soon after Muzo was placed under government control, the Chivor mine was rediscovered on the basis of a description written almost 300 years earlier. In 1888, Colombian mining engineer Don Francisco Restrepo found a manuscript dating back to the early seventeenth century in a Dominican convent in Quito, Ecuador. This manuscript, written by Fray Martin de Aguado, described the location of the Chivor mine as the only place in the Andes where one could see through a pass in the moun-

Figure 3-6. *A view looking to the north over the Muzo mines. Photo by Peter C. Keller.*

tains to the plains of the Orinoco. Restrepo's search for the legendary mine ended successfully in 1896. Although legal problems with the government hampered Restrepo's early mining activities, his early twentieth-century partnership with German mining engineer Fritz Klein coincided with the lifting of some of these restrictions and promising production at the mine. When World War I broke out, however, Klein returned to Germany for military service. Restrepo died at Chivor, and, with Germany's defeat, Klein lost all rights to the mine as a result of alien property legislation. In 1919, Chivor was purchased by the Colombian Emerald Syndicate, Ltd., a U.S. company. Since then it has changed hands many times, with varying degrees of success, and has been managed by such notable mining engineers as Peter W. Rainier (Rainier, 1942) and Willis Bronkie. The Chivor mines are currently in the hands of the Quintero family.

In 1953, a new mine was discovered 8 km southwest of Chivor at Gachalá, reportedly when a woodcutter's mule uncovered an emerald-bearing rock (Anderton, 1955). Although the mine has produced only sporadically since 1953, in 1967 an 858-carat crystal, generally considered one of the finest in existence, was found there. The 5-cm hexagonal prism, known simply as the Gachalá emerald, is housed in the Smithsonian Institution (Trapp, 1969).

Recent History and Production

Emerald mining under government control has been a questionable business proposition. In 1946, the government entrusted the management of the Muzo mines, including the power to regulate all mining and marketing of emeralds from that district, to Banco de la República (Feininger, 1970). However, illicit emerald mining and dealing continued to be widespread, with an estimated loss to the government of more than 28 million pesos during the period 1946 to 1969, when the bank relinquished control of the Muzo emeralds to the Empresa Colombiana de Minas (ECOMINAS), the government's mining agency. The situation at Muzo then worsened, to the point that in 1973 more than 900 people were killed in feuds, and the mines were forced to close. The mines stayed officially closed until 1977, when the government solicited bids for 5-year leases on the Muzo mines, the Coscuez mine, and the Peñas Blancas mine. After extensive negotiations, the Muzo lease was awarded to the Sociedad Minera Boyacense Ltda., the Coscuez lease went to Esmeraldas y Minas de Colombia, S.A. (ESMERACOL), and the Peñas Blancas lease went to the Quintero brothers, who also control the Chivor mine (Colombia American Business, 1979). Today, Muzo is considered the most important emerald mine in the world (Fig. 3-6).

Figure 3-7. Looking eastward at guaqueros working in the Río Itoco below the main mining operation at Muzo. Photo by Peter C. Keller.

Unfortunately, 5-year leases of Muzo encouraged the lessees to mine the area as rapidly as possible, and their methods were not as conservative of resources as they should be. When I visited Muzo in 1979 and again in 1980, the main area was being worked harshly with bulldozers and dynamite, a method not adopted in the past because of the fragility of the emeralds. After an area has been blasted, bulldozers scrape off the overburden until the white calcite veins are exposed. Then, teams are brought in to work each vein with pick and shovel. When emeralds are found, they are placed in a canvas bag for sorting by the mine lessees each evening. These sorted parcels are then sealed and taken to Bogotá for further grading and subsequent marketing.

Because the main mine area was being stripped away so rapidly, a significant portion of the potential emerald production was lost to the gravels of the Río Itoco, with the result that an estimated 15,000 guaqueros (independent miners, directly translated as "treasure hunters") mine the riverbed each day (Figs. 3-7 and 3-8).

Currently, the government has leased the Muzo property to two companies, Tecminas and Coehminas, under a series of 10-year leases, and

Figure 3-8. Guaqueros at Muzo. Photo by Peter C. Keller.

Figure 3-9. View of current mining activity at Muzo. Photo by Peter C. Keller.

the situation there has improved dramatically (Fig. 3-9). The government is very concerned with the ecology of the area, and the new leaseholders are doing a great deal to cooperate. Most important is the development of underground mining at Muzo to replace the wholesale strip-mining of the mountainside. The development of two major shafts and four tunnels is progressing well, with economic success for the mining companies involved.

Geology of the Muzo and Chivor Emerald Districts

Studies of the geology of Muzo and, to a lesser extent, Chivor tell how the emeralds occur and where to direct future exploration, but a detailed study of the Eastern Cordillera has thus far been inhibited by the rugged terrain and thick vegetation that have also restricted exploration.

The Colombian Andes consist of three subparallel ranges: the Western, or Cordillera Occidental; the Central, or Cordillera Central; and the Eastern, or Cordillera Oriental. According to Clements (1941), the Western and Central ranges consist primarily of granites and are best known for their gold deposits and production. The Eastern range, however, consists mostly of sedimentary units, principally limestones and shales with minor igneous and metamorphic rocks exposed only locally. Clements places a Paleozoic age on these crystalline rocks.

The major emerald deposits are limited to the eastern (Chivor) and western (Muzo) margins of the Cordillera Oriental where Cretaceous sediments are well exposed. The geology of the Muzo district has been described well by Pogue (1916), Lleras (1929), Scheibe (1933), Clements (1941), and Oppenheim (1948), who agree that emeralds are restricted to the Lower Cretaceous Villeta formation, a great

Figure 3-10. Emeralds at Muzo are confined to calcite veins in the carbonaceous shale. This miner works a vein exposed by bulldozing and blasting. Photo by Peter C. Keller.

thickness of intensely folded and fractured black carbonaceous shale and minor limestones. The black shale is so rich in carbon that handling it invariably soils one's hands. The Lower Cretaceous age of the Villeta has been determined from the presence of fossil ammonites. The highly fractured shales have been invaded by numerous white calcite fracture-filling veins, and it is in these veins that the emeralds occur (Fig. 3-10). Dolomite, quartz, pyrite, and parisite, an uncommon rare earth calcium carbonate, are accessory minerals commonly found with emerald in these veins. Lleras (1929), Scheibe (1933), and Oppenheim (1948) noted albite as a common vein mineral at Muzo, but Clements (1941) did not observe albite, nor did I.

Lleras (1929) divided the Villeta formation into two members, namely, the Cambiado and the overlying Emerald Beds. The lower member at Muzo, the Cambiado, consists of highly folded, faulted, and fractured carbonaceous shales and thinly bed-

ded limestones. The Cambiado is discordantly overlain by the Emerald Beds, the latter consisting of thinly bedded, weathered, yellowish gray shales that have also been intensely folded and invaded by thin calcite veins. The Emerald Beds, as the name implies, contain localized concentrations of emeralds associated with calcite, dolomite, pyrite, quartz, and parisite. Locally, the Cambiado and Emerald Beds are separated by two thin agglomeratic layers of calcite crystals designated the Cama and the overlying Cenicero (Oppenheim, 1948). The major difference between these two layers appears to be textural. The Cama consists of an agglomerate of relatively large calcite crystals, whereas the Cenicero, which is usually about a meter thick, consists of small calcite crystals along with pyrite in a carbonate ground mass. Barite has also been reported in the Cenicero (Oppenheim, 1948).

The sedimentary rock units at Chivor are somewhat different lithologically from those described for Muzo, but the geology is basically the same. At Chivor, such units are almost entirely shales and argillites, with minor limestone and sandstone (Rainier, 1929). The general geology and stratigraphy of this area are not as well known as at Muzo. The stratigraphic section at Chivor appears to consist primarily of at least 1,000 m of conformable sediments. Johnson (1961) provides a good description of these sediments and the geology. Johnson indicates that the emerald zone at Chivor runs about 10 km east to west and about 5 km north to south. Fossil ammonites, bivalves, and ferns indicate that the sediments of the district are Cretaceous. As at Muzo, these sediments are heavily faulted and folded. They are mostly shales and argillites with some blocks or floaters of carbonaceous limestone present near the top of the stratigraphic section. The most prominent unit is a poorly cemented yellowish shale that overlies a thick sequence of gray-blue shales and argillites. No emeralds have been reported from the yellowish shale cap; most occur in a blue-gray argillite about midway through the section. Johnson (1961) suggests that the occurrence of emeralds at Chivor is structurally related, as if the emerald veins were concentrated along the axes of tight folds in the argillites. He states: "If a vein is discovered traveling in the trough of a syncline, the production of stones may be immense."

Chivor emeralds are found mostly in veins, but in rare instances they may occur in cavities, as was the case with the famous Patricia emerald. The cavities, when present, are always associated with the veins. The veins run parallel to the bedding of the sediments, which suggests that separations between bedding laminae provided the avenues of least resistance for fissure-filling hydrothermal solutions that crystallized to form veins. Such veins occur up to 15 cm in thickness but rarely exceed 65 m in length. Emeralds commonly are found where two veins intersect. Johnson (1961) divided the veins into three mineralogical types: pyrite, albite, and pyrite with albite. The mineralization is in sharp contrast to the emerald-bearing veins of Muzo, where the gem material occurs in white calcite, dolomite, or both.

Three more or less parallel iron bands, consisting of pyrite and limonite, appear about 50 m apart from one another, interlaminated in the stratigraphic section at Chivor. These bands appear to control the distribution of emeralds to some extent. Emeralds are most prevalent below the lowest of the three iron bands or between the lowest and middle bands. Very few emeralds have been reported above the middle or upper iron bands. This distribution suggests that these bands may have acted as impervious dams for the rising emerald-bearing solutions.

Important Colombian Emeralds

Even though emeralds have been mined in Colombia since pre-Columbian times, relatively few very fine large examples are known today. Because of the extremely high value of faceted stones, fine large emerald crystals are particularly rare.

During the seventeenth century, large Colombian emeralds were eagerly sought by the Mogul nobility of India. By way of Spain, a great many of the early Colombian stones found a ready market in India through well-established trade routes. One particularly fine example of these emeralds is the Mogul, which is currently owned by the private collector Allan Caplan. The Mogul emerald measures 5 cm by 3.8 cm by 3.5 cm and weighs 217.8 carats (Caplan, 1968). The front of the stone is carved with the floral motif typical of Mogul carvers; the back contains an Islamic prayer and the date 1695 A.D. The drilled stone was probably worn on an article of clothing, perhaps a turban (Fig. 3-11).

Many of these Colombian emeralds were taken from India in 1739 during the sacking of Delhi by the Persians and became part of the crown jewels of Iran in Tehran. More than 1,000 of these emeralds were examined and it was reported that most were over 10 carats and some exceeded 300 carats (Meen and Tushingham, 1968). Certainly this collection and the collection in the Topkapi Museum in Istanbul, Turkey, must be considered the two largest collections of Colombian emeralds in the world.

One of the most spectacular pieces of emerald jewelry on public display in the United States is the 300-year-old Spanish Inquisition necklace, which is in the Smithsonian Institution's collection. This necklace was reportedly worn in Spanish and, later, French courts. The drilled hexagonal and cylindrical beads that make up the necklace may very well have originally belonged to articles of pre-Columbian jewelry and were simply reset into this magnificent piece. A 24-mm by 15-mm drilled emerald bead forms the focal point of the necklace; in addition, 14 smaller emerald beads average 16 mm by 7 mm. Dunn (1975) reports that the necklace also contains more than 360 mine-cut diamonds, 16 of which must be considered major gems themselves. These 16 large diamonds have also been drilled.

Another spectacular Colombian emerald in the Smithsonian collection is the 75-carat square-cut stone in the Hooker brooch, originally worn as a

Figure 3-11. *During the Spanish conquest of Colombia, many fine emeralds were sent back to India, where Mogul nobility had them fashioned into jewelry. This 217.8-carat emerald from the Allan Caplan collection, known as the Mogul, exhibits beautiful craftsmanship. The floral motif on one side is typical of Mogul art; the Islamic prayer written in Arabic on the other side includes a date equivalent to 1695 A.D. Photo by Harold and Erica Van Pelt.*

Figure 3-12. *The 75-carat Hooker emerald, once part of a sultan's belt buckle, is remarkably free of the inclusions normally associated with such large stones from Muzo, Colombia. Photo by Dane Penland courtesy of the National Museum of Natural History, Smithsonian Institution, Washington, D.C. (NMNH #G7719).*

Turkish Sultan's belt buckle. This stone is particularly significant because it lacks the internal flaws typical of large emeralds (Desautels, 1979) (Fig. 3-12).

Fine, large emerald crystals are very rare in nature and, because of their inherent value as cut stones, rarely survive intact in the marketplace. However, a few are worth noting. Reputedly, one of the finest Colombian emerald crystals in the world is not from Muzo or Chivor, but rather from the recently discovered Gachalá mine. This fine hexagonal prism weighs 858 carats and is of unusually fine color and luster. It, too, is part of the gem collection at the Smithsonian Institution (Trapp, 1969).

Several emerald crystals have acquired names through the years. The most famous, perhaps, is the 632-carat Patricia emerald, which was discovered in December 1920 at the Chivor mine by Justo Daza, who received a $10 bonus for finding the crystal. The Patricia is the largest known emerald from Chivor and was sold early in 1921 for $60,000. According to Johnson (1961), the blast that uncovered the Patricia destroyed a pocket that, when examined, contained fragments of an emerald crystal that was probably even larger. The Patricia was donated to the American Museum of Natural History in the early 1950s.

Another named crystal is the famous Devonshire emerald, which was loaned to the British Museum of Natural History in 1936. The current whereabouts of the stone are unknown; the curator of the museum's gem collection recently verified that the museum has only a wax model. In 1936, the 1384-carat Devonshire emerald was the largest known emerald from the Muzo mine. Reportedly, the Devonshire is so named because it was given by Pedro I, Emperor of Brazil, to the sixth Duke of Devonshire sometime after 1831, when Pedro I was forced to leave Brazil for Europe. The simple hexagonal prism is approximately 5 cm by 5 cm. It is pictured in Tremayne (1936).

The size and importance of the Patricia and Devonshire emerald crystals are somewhat overshadowed by the collection of unnamed crystals housed in the basement vaults of the Banco de la República in Bogotá. This collection consists of five crystals ranging in size from 220 carats to 1795.88

Figure 3-13. The finest specimen in the collection of the Banco de la República is this exceptional 1,759-carat crystal from Muzo, Colombia. Photo by Harold and Erica Van Pelt.

carats. The finest is an extraordinary 1759-carat crystal with excellent color and crystal form (Fig. 3-13). All of the crystals are reportedly from Muzo and were probably found between 1947 and 1969, when the bank controlled the mines, although their history is not well documented. These crystals are not on public display in Colombia.

The largest known single emerald crystal from Colombia is the 7025-carat Emilia crystal discovered in 1969. Reportedly from the Las Cruces mine (near Gachalá), it is owned by a private mining concern. It has been displayed at expositions around the world, although its current whereabouts are unknown.

Many fine emeralds from the colonial period of Colombia's history are found in its church treasures. The finest of these treasures, now on display in the Museo del Oro in Bogotá, is the Custodia de San Ignacio or La Lechuga. This magnificent piece contains over 1,480 emeralds (Fig. 3-14).

Figure 3-14. In the sixteenth and seventeenth centuries, wealthy landowners in Colombia paid their respects to the Roman Catholic Church by commissioning incredible altar pieces fashioned from gold and studded with emeralds and other precious stones. Today, one of the most extraordinary church treasures remaining in Colombia is this Custodia de San Ignacio or "La Lechuga," which consists of approximately 8.5 kg of gold and more than 1,480 emeralds. Photo by Harold and Erica Van Pelt.

REFERENCES

Anderton, R. W. 1950. Report on Chivor emerald mine. *Gems & Gemology* 6:276–277.

Anderton, R. W. 1955. The new Gachala emerald mine in Colombia. *Gems & Gemology* 8:195–196.

Anderton, R. 1965. The present status of Colombian emerald mining. *Lapidary Journal* 19:374–377.

Ball, S. H. 1931. Historical notes on gem mining. *Econ. Geol.* 26:681–738.

Bancroft, P. 1971. The lure of Chivor. *Lapidary Journal*, 15:128–131.

Barriga Villalba, A. M., and A. M. Barriga del Diestro. 1973. *La esmeralda de Colombia.* Colegio Mayor de Nuestra Senora del Rosario, Bogota.

Bowersox, G. W. 1985. A status report on gemstones from Afghanistan. *Gems & Gemology* 21(4):192–204.

Bray, W. 1978. *The Gold of El Dorado.* London Times, Ltd., London.

Caplan, A. 1968. An important carved emerald from the Mogul period of India. *Lapidary Journal* 22:1336–1337.

Clements, T. 1941. The emerald mines of Muzo, Colombia. *Gems & Gemology* 3:130–133.

Colombian American Business. 1979. Colombian emeralds: The little green stone questions. *Colombian American Business* 18:3–5.

Copeland, L. L. 1950. Emerald mine report from Colombia. *Gems & Gemology* 6:316.

Desautels, P. E. 1979. *The Gem Collection.* Smithsonian Institution Press, Washington, D.C.

Dominguez, A. R. A. 1965. *Historia de las esmeraldas de Colombia.* Impreso en Graficos Ducal, Bogota. 297 pages.

Dunn, P. 1975. Emeralds in the Smithsonian gem collection. *Lapidary Journal* 29:1572–1575.

Feininger, T. 1970. Emerald mining in Colombia: History and geology. *Mineralogical Record* 1.142–149.

Johnson, P. W. 1961. The Chivor emerald mine. *Journal of Gemology* 8:126–152.

Keller, P. C. 1981. Emeralds of Colombia. *Gems & Gemology* 17(2):80–92.

Keller, P. C. 1983. The Capao Topaz deposit, Ouro Prêto, Minas Gerais, Brazil. *Gems & Gemology* 19(1):12–20.

Klein, I. 1941. *Smaragde unter dem Urwald.* Oswald Arnold, Berlin. 285 pages.

Lleras, C. R. 1929. Minas de esmeraldas. *Boletin de Minas y Petroleos* 1(1).

Louderback, G. E. 1907. Benitoite, a new California gem mineral. *Bulletin of the Dept. of Geology, Univ. of California* 5(9).

MacFadden, C. R. 1934. Emerald mining in Colombia. *Gems & Gemology* 1:149–154.

Meen, V. B., and A. D. Tushingham. 1968. *Crown Jewels of Iran.* University of Toronto Press, Toronto.

Olsen, D. R. 1971. Origin of topaz deposits near Ouro Prêto, Minas Gerais, Brazil. *Econ. Geol.* 66(4):627–631.

Oppenheim, V. 1948. The Muzo emerald zone, Colombia, S.A. *Econ. Geol.* 43:31–38.

Pogue, J. 1916. The emerald deposits of Muzo, Colombia. *Transactions of the American Institute of Mining and Metallurgical Engineers* 55:810–834.

Rainier, P. W. 1929. *The Chivor-Somondoco emerald mines of Colombia.* Technical Publication 258. American Institute of Mining and Metallurgical Engineers, New York.

Rainier, P. W. 1942. *Green Fire.* Random House, New York.

Ringsrud, R. 1986. The Coscuez mine: a major source of Colombian emeralds. *Gems & Gemology* 22:67–79.

Scalisi, P., and D. Cook. 1983. *Classic Mineral Localities of the World: Asia and Australia.* Van Nostrand Reinhold, New York, 226 pages.

Scheibe, R. 1933. Informe geologico sobre la mina de esmeraldas de Muzo. *Compilacion de los Estudios Geologicos Oficiales en Colombia* 1:169–198.

Sinkankas, J. 1981. *Emerald and other Bryls.* Chilton Book Company, Radnor, Pa. 665 pages.

Switzer, G. 1948. Recent emerald mine, Colombia. *Gems & Gemology* 6:25–26.

Tenhagen, J. W. 1972. Muzo emerald mine, Colombia. *Gems & Gemology* 14:77–81.

Trapp, F. W. 1969. The Gachalá emerald shares the spotlight with the Hope diamond at the Smithsonian. *Lapidary Journal* 23:628.

Tremayne, A. 1936. The Devonshire emerald in Natural History Museum. *Gemmologist* 6:98–99.

Wokittel, R. 1960. Esmeralda Colombia Instituto Geologico Nacional, Seccion de Geologia Economica.

4

Gemstones Formed in Pegmatites:
Gem Pegmatites of Minas Gerais, Brazil

Of all the rock types encountered on Earth, none is more gemologically important for its variety and quantity of gemstones than the igneous bodies known as *pegmatites.* More gemstones are found in pegmatites than in any other type of deposit. Pegmatites yield huge quantities of tourmaline, beryl (aquamarine and morganite), chrysoberyl, kunzite, and topaz, as well as a host of much rarer gems and minerals. Important descriptions of pegmatites are found in Sinkankas (1981) and Schneiderhohn (1961).

According to Shigley and Kampf (1984), the term *pegmatite* was coined in the early 1800s by the French mineralogist Hauy to describe the geometric intergrowth of feldspar, quartz, and mica that petrologists today call *graphic granite.* Generally speaking, a pegmatite is a dikelike body of once molten rock that characteristically contains very large crystals and may contain rare minerals. Compositionally, a wide variety of rock types may be considered pegmatitic, but by far the most common are identical to that of granite and are therefore known as *granitic pegmatites.* These granitic pegmatites are made up mostly of quartz, potassium-feldspar, and muscovite mica. Except for some rare instances of corundum-bearing pegmatites in Tanzania (Solesbury, 1967) and Kashmir (Atkinson and Kothavala, 1983; Middlemiss, 1931), all gem-bearing pegmatites are granitic. The rare corundum-bearing pegmatites appear to be quartz poor, consisting principally of acid feldspars. The formation of these unusual pegmatites is still unclear, but one theory is that they were granitic pegmatites that were stripped of silica by the surrounding rocks, which allowed for the formation of corundum.

Gem minerals are the result of the incorporation into the pegmatite of rare elements that are unable to fit into the crystal structure of the quartz, feldspar, and mica that make up the bulk of the pegmatite. These rare elements include beryllium, lithium, boron, manganese, phosphorous, and fluorine. Texturally, these crystals are highly variable in size and much larger than their enclosing rock. The pegmatite minerals usually increase in size from the outer chill margins, which may be measured in millimeters, to the interior core in which crystals up to many meters long may be found (Cameron et al., 1949). According to Jahns (1953), logs of beryl and spodumene up to 15 meters long have been found in the Etta and Keystone pegmatites in the Black Hills of South Dakota (Page et al., 1953). Similar occurrences have been noted in the Ural Mountains of the Soviet Union, and the famous Harding pegmatite in Taos County, New Mexico. Gem crystals are much smaller, but crystals of topaz, aquamarine, and tourmaline weighing many tens of kilograms have been recovered in Minas Gerais, Brazil. One of the most famous aquamarine crystals is a 110.5-kg crystal discovered in 1910 at the Papamal mine. In 1954 a 34.7-kg aquamarine prism was found near Topazio. In 1978 an incredible pocket of rubellite was recovered in the Itatiaia (Jonas) mine; among its many record-size crystals was the 135-kg rocket.

Heinrich (1956) classified pegmatites into three types based on their internal structure:

1. Simple pegmatites that consist only of quartz, feldspar, and mica and exhibit no internal structure. This is the most common class.
2. Zoned pegmatites that consist of not only quartz, feldspar, and mica but also a variety of accessory minerals. These minerals exhibit distinct zoning with crystal size increasing toward the pegmatite's center or core. The zones ideally are reflected as concentric layers around a very coarse-grained core. These zones or layers include the border, wall, intermediate, and core zones. Gemstones may be present in the core or intermediate zones.
3. Complex pegmatites that are very similar to zoned pegmatites but have undergone extensive alteration. Often they contain an extensive array of rare minerals, including gemstones that may form in irregular openings or pockets, which may vary greatly in size up to several meters. Pockets are found in the central core or at the edge of the core and the intermediate zone.

More recently, geologists have attempted to reclassify pegmatites based on the depth that they formed below the surface (Ginzburg et al., 1979; Cerny, 1982). Four classes of pegmatites have been recognized:

1. Those formed at depths greater than 11 km, which tend to be unzoned and consist of only quartz, feldspar, and mica.
2. Those found at depths between 7 and 11 km, which may be zoned but are still of basic composition.
3. Those formed at depths between 3.5 and 7 km, which may be zoned and contain rare minerals and pockets of small crystals.
4. Those formed at depths less than 3.5 km, which are zoned and may contain larger crystals and pockets of rare minerals, including gemstones.

Based on this method of classification, the pegmatites that formed at relatively shallow depths below the earth's surface are those of gemological importance. These pegmatites are usually associated with intrusive granitic batholiths that regionally make up the cores of mountains or, if exposed, rounded, rolling topography. The shallow, zoned pegmatites are usually sheetlike in shape and fill fractures in the preexisting rock that surrounds them.

The granitic pegmatites' usually high concentration of rare and gem minerals is a function of its very unusual mode of formation. Geologists have argued over how pegmatites formed for many years but today agree that the zoned and complex pegmatites have formed from a granitic magma at shallow depths. The classic work on the origin of pegmatites is that of Fersman (1931), whose model has been refined by Jahns (1953, 1955) and Jahns and Burnham (1969). A remarkable series of events leads up to the concentration of rare elements and subsequent formation of gemstones in pegmatites. During the final stages of crystallization of a granitic magma, magma rich in rare elements and volatiles flows up from the large, partially solid magma and is injected into fractures in the preexisting rocks (Fig. 4-1). Water is the most important of the volatiles. The rare elements include beryllium, lithium, boron, phosphorous, fluorine, and cesium. As the pegmatitic fluids cool, quartz, feldspar, and mica crystallize along the outer edge next to the wall rock to form a relatively fine-grained border and wall zones. The border zone acts as an insulator against heat loss and allows the rest of the pegmatitic fluids to cool more slowly and form larger crystals. As a result, the wall and intermediate zones, which form next, are made up of larger crystals of quartz, potassium-rich feldspars, and mica, along with some rarer minerals such as beryl and spodumene. The remaining fluids are now highly enriched with the rare elements that have not fit into the crystal structure of the common quartz, feldspar, and mica. The granitic magma is now almost totally crystallized, leaving behind only trapped pockets of fluids rich in rare elements. With continued cooling, these pockets begin to

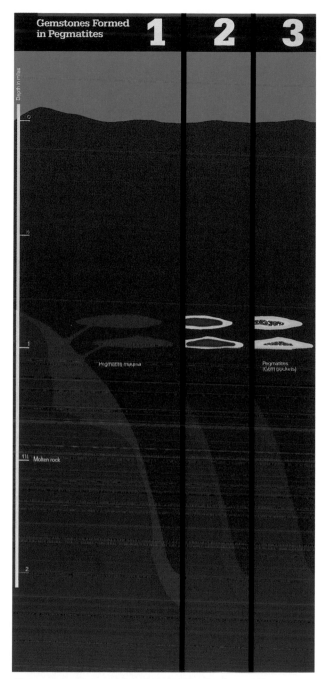

Figure 4-1. *Digram showing pegmatite formation.
Courtesy of the Natural History Museum of Los Angeles
County.*

erside Counties of California (Jahns and Wright,
1951; Jahns, 1954, 1979); the Alto-Ligonha area,
Mozambique (Hutchinson and Claus, 1956; Neiva
and Neves, 1960); the Kleine Spitzkopje and other
pegmatites in Namibia; Madagascar (Murdock,
1963); the Ural Mountains, Ukraine, and the Chita
area of the Soviet Union (Sinkankas, 1981); and,
most recently, Jos, Nigeria, and the Nuistan area of
Afghanistan (Bariand and Poullen, 1978; Bowersox,
1985). Significant gem-bearing pegmatites occur in
the states of Rio Grande do Norte, Bahia, Goiás, and
Espírito Santo, Brazil. Many of these have only recently been exploited.

PEGMATITES OF MINAS GERAIS, BRAZIL

The world's most important gemstone-producing
pegmatites are in the northeastern portion of the
state of Minas Gerais, Brazil (Fig. 4-2). The most
comprehensive overviews of these deposits are
found in Sinkankas (1981) and in a series of articles
by Proctor (1984, 1985a, 1985b). In this huge pegmatite district, perhaps more gem tourmaline,

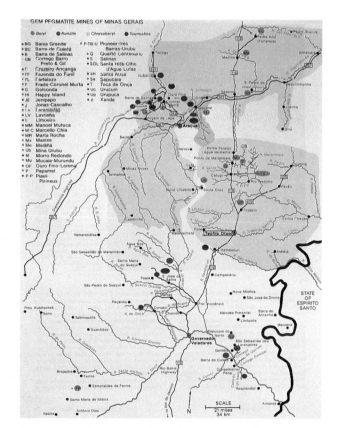

Figure 4-2. *Gem pegmatite mines of Minas Gerais,
Brazil. (Proctor, 1984). Courtesy of the Gemological
Institute of America.*

crystallize as quartz, feldspar, rare minerals, and
gem crystals such as tourmaline, topaz, kunzite,
morganite, and aquamarine. These crystals are typically found projecting into the center of the
pocket.

Granitic pegmatites are extremely numerous
worldwide, but only a small percentage are gem
bearing. The most important gem-bearing pegmatitic districts are found in the San Diego and Riv-

Figure 4-3. The pegmatites of Brazil have produced an extraordinary array of gemstones, including tourmaline, topaz, kunzite, aquamarine, and morganite. This collection of Brazilian gems is part of the Trelawney collection of the Natural History Museum of Los Angeles County. Photo by Harold and Erica Van Pelt.

topaz, kunzite, morganite, aquamarine, and chrysoberyl have been recovered in this century than from the rest of the pegmatites in the world combined (Fig. 4-3). In 1676 the Portuguese explorer Fernao Dias Paes Leme discovered the first gem-bearing pegmatites near what is today called the Cruzeiro mine. This discovery went largely unnoticed due to a lack of appreciation for pegmatite gemstones in the European market of the time. In the latter half of the nineteenth century, large numbers of German and Lebanese immigrants migrating to the pegmatite region of Minas Gerais discovered the pegmatitic gems. They soon established a close trading relationship with the famous gem-cutting center at Idar-Oberstein, Germany.

The gem trade was largely limited to the German market until World War II. With World War II, commercial interest in pegmatites shifted to the great need for strategic pegmatite minerals such as quartz, lithium minerals, and mica. Geologists scoured the Brazilian countryside in search of these badly needed strategic materials, and the discovery of widespread gem deposits was a by-product that was not appreciated until after the war (Pecora et al., 1950a,b). With peace, commercial interests shifted back to the gemstones, this time on a much greater scale.

Since World War II, the former mica-producing centers of Governador Valadares and Teófilo Otoni have become the gem mining centers of today. The capital of Minas Gerais, Belo Horizonte, is a major cutting and marketing center. Currently, the most important gem pegmatite districts are the Cruzeiro, Golconda, and Virgem da Lapa.

Geology of the Minas Gerais Pegmatite Belt

Rough terrain, difficult access, and, most importantly, deep chemical weathering have hampered detailed studies of the regional geology of Minas Gerais. All rocks in the region have been intensely weathered, most to a depth of 30 meters or more, producing thick lateritic soil horizons that typically shroud the underlying rocks of Minas Gerais (Fig. 4-4). Regional correlation of rock units has been particularly difficult. As a result, very little geologic work on a broad scale has been done. Only recently has a geologic map of the state been published (Da Costa and Romano, 1976).

Of the geologic work on the pegmatite region of Minas Gerais undertaken during World War II, one of the most important efforts, the result of several years of regional mapping, was published by Pecora and associates (1950a). Their work revealed a Precambrian basement complex, which was designated the Complexo Fundamental. They assigned a tremendous variety of rock types to this unit, including biotite schists interlayered with amphibolite schists and quartzites, banded and granitoid gneisses, and biotite-garnet schists, and observed that the gem-bearing (mica) pegmatites are found principally in areas that are underlain by the Complexo Fundamental.

The Complexo Fundamental is unconformably overlain by a series of Precambrian metasediments designated the Minas series. The Minas series consists mostly of a sericitic phyllite. These rocks were later intruded by granitic batholiths that metamorphosed, domed, and fractured the sediments to provide channels for the pegmatitic fluids that accompanied the magmas of subsequent intrusive activity.

The Minas series is overlain by the much folded and faulted Itacolomy series of predominantly phyllites and quartzites of late Precambrian age. The Itacolomy series has also been intruded by pegmatites, suggesting that pegmatite-related magmatic activity continued for some time following the deposition of this unit. The conglomerates, phyllites, and sandstones of the overlying early Paleozoic Lavas and Silurian age Baubue series do not contain pegmatites, and, therefore, areas underlain by these younger units are of no commercial interest.

The pegmatites have been more accurately dated by Dirac and Ebert (1967). They determined

Figure 4-4. A garimpeiro works a pocket at the Salinas mine after gem material was spotted when the bulldozer made its most recent pass. On the right wall, the sharp contact between the kaolin of the pegmatite and the red lateritic soil that covers it is evident. Photo by Keith Proctor, 1985.

that the approximate age of the gem-bearing pegmatites is 490 million years. During this time, pegmatitic fluids and granitic magmas domed and fractured the overlying rocks and invaded the newly created passageways. With time, these fluids cooled and crystallized to form dikes in the older metamorphic rocks. Subsequent intense weathering and rapid erosion exposed and destroyed many of the pegmatites and left the more durable minerals, including gemstones, to be concentrated in drainage basins as alluvial deposits. The great granitic batholiths have been exhumed and create a landscape of rounded mountains called *inselbergs* ("island mountains"), the most famous of which is Sugarloaf in Rio de Janeiro.

Today, thousands of gem-bearing pegmatites in varying degrees of alteration are known in Minas

Figure 4-5. The entire village of Cruzeiro (note the cross in the foreground, from which both the village and the mine get their name) is pictured here, isolated along this ridge of the Serra Safira. Photo by Peter C. Keller.

Figure 4-6. Open-pit mining at the top of the Cruzeiro mine. Note the two tunnels that follow the vein underground into the quartzite wall. Photo by Peter C. Keller.

Gerais. Many of these pegmatites have been studied individually, and the literature is rich with their descriptions. The most important and best known of these are the Cruzeiro, Golconda, Virgem da Lapa, and Itatiaia (Jonas) pegmatites.

The Cruzeiro mine is one of the largest and most consistent producers of fine green tourmaline in the world. It is located about 80 km northwest of Governador Valadares, on the eastern slope of the Serra Safira, a major north-south mountain range dividing the Río Suacui Grande and its tributary, the Río Urupuca. Cruzeiro was a major producer of mica in both world wars, including about 12 percent of Brazil's mica production during World War II (Cassedanne and Sauer, 1980).

Cruzeiro (Fig. 4-5) consists of three pegmatite bodies that strike N20°W in a white to pinkish medium-grained quartzite belonging to the Complexo Fundamental (Fig. 4-6). The pegmatites are all excellent examples of the complex zoned pegmatites described by Shigley and Kampf (1984). Since World War II, the Cruzeiro mine is most famous for its production of emerald green tourmaline and fine blue indicolite, including world-famous specimens such as the approximately 35-cm-high green tourmaline on quartz belonging to the Natural History Museum of Los Angeles County (Fig. 4-7). This specimen is probably from a pocket discovered in 1968 that produced approximately 2,000 kilograms of opaque but very aesthetic crystals (Proctor, 1985b).

The Golconda district consists of three mines, designated Golconda I, II, and III, which have produced an abundance of fine green and bicolored pink-and-green tourmalines. The district is located approximately 34 km northwest of Governador Va-

ladares. One of the oldest mica producers in Brazil, it began production in 1908 (Pecora et al., 1950b) and supplied mica for both world wars.

According to Pecora et al. (1950b), the Golconda pegmatite is a nearly horizontal sheetlike body ranging from 3 to 11 meters in thickness. It has intruded a mica schist that probably belongs to the Complexo Fundamental and is also a classic example of a complex granitic pegmatite with distinct zoning. Gem pockets are common in the core zone and contain tantalite, albite, cassiterite, microlite, cookeite, and muscovite, along with tourmaline, garnet, and beryl.

Current mining in the Golconda district is heavily mechanized, and extensive underground workings are being developed, with fresh memories of past glory (Fig. 4-8). According to Proctor (1985b), the Golconda III mine has produced "literally millions of carats of fine blue-green, green, and rose-colored tourmaline, between 1961 and 1967."

The Virgem da Lapa pegmatite district, located approximately 34 km west-northwest of Araçuaí, is one of the most famous of Brazil's pegmatites to the mineral collector (Proctor, 1985a). In the 1970s, Virgem da Lapa produced extraordinary amounts of tourmaline, aquamarine, and blue topaz crystals, which were ranked as some of the world's finest (Cassedanne and Lowell, 1982) (Fig. 4-9). The district consists of a group of mines working a series of nearly horizontal tabular or lens-shaped complex granitic pegmatites. The Virgem da Lapa pegmatites are especially noteworthy for their relatively unaltered condition, which possibly explains the high quality of the mineral specimens they yield.

Figure 4-7. *One of the finest tourmaline specimens ever produced from the Cruzeiro mine is this approximately 40-cm-high green tourmaline on quartz. This exceptional specimen is from the Natural History Museum of Los Angeles County. Photo by Harold and Erica Van Pelt.*

Figure 4-8. The Golconda tourmaline mine, Minas Gerais, Brazil, is one of Brazil's most mechanized. Here, bulldozers are used to move the overburden and waste from the mine entrance. Photo by Keith Proctor (1984).

Figure 4-9. This unusually fine, 21-cm-high blue topaz crystal, with a coating of lepidolite, is from the Virgem da Lapa area of Minas Gerais, Brazil. It is part of the Smithsonian Institution's collection. Photo by Harold and Erica Van Pelt.

Figure 4-10. Gem tourmaline crystal from the Jonas mine in Minas Gerais, Brazil. This superb specimen is known as the "Rose of Itatiaia" and is in the collection of K. Proctor. Photo by Harold and Erica Van Pelt.

Another pegmatite that is particularly familiar to the mineral collector is the Itatiaia or Jonas mine. In 1978 this relatively unaltered pegmatite yielded a pocket containing hundreds of kilograms of fine cranberry red tourmalines, some of extraordinary size (Fig. 4-10). Proctor (1985b) provides a superb description of this pocket, along with an artist's re-creation of what it must have looked like. The Itatiaia pegmatite is located just southeast of Governador Valadares. The nearly vertical pegmatite is about 200 meters long and 23 meters wide and extends from depth to the surface. It is typically zoned but noteworthy for its abundance of black schorl crystals.

Mining Techniques

Garimpeiros, or independent miners, are the backbone of the gem-mining industry in Minas Gerais (Fig. 4-11). A few more sophisticated mining operations utilize relatively up-to-date equipment such as jackhammers, compressors, and bulldozers, but most mining is done with the tools of the garimpeiros, picks, shovels, and carbide lamps. The garimpeiros work as individuals or in small groups, usually digging into the soft, deeply kaolinized pegmatites.

According to Proctor (1984), federal law dictates that all the gem deposits belong to the government and any licensed garimpeiro may work on any state-owned land or private lands, assuming consent of the owner. The garimpeiro must pay between 10 and 50 percent royalty to the landowner. These garimpeiros are generally migratory,

working wherever they believe gems may be present. According to Proctor (1984), the garimpeiro force is dwindling as those workers go to work in more productive and steady employment.

Noteworthy Brazilian Pegmatite Gems

Because pegmatites are known for their abundance of extraordinarily large crystals, that they have provided the world's museums with some of their largest crystals and faceted gemstones is not surprising (Figs. 4-12 through 4-15). Brazilian gemstones larger than a thousand carats are not unusual. The gem collection of the Smithsonian Institution includes a 2,054-carat greenish gold beryl, a 1,363-carat green beryl, a 1,000-carat aquamarine, and a 911-carat aquamarine. Their morganites or pink-orange beryls are somewhat smaller at 330 and 235.5 carats. The Smithsonian

Figure 4-11. The garimpeiro is the independent miner making up the backbone of Brazil's gem-mining industry. Photo by Peter C. Keller.

Figure 4-12. Gem aquamarine crystal from Minas Gerais, Brazil. Photo by Harold and Erica Van Pelt.

Figure 4-13. Rough and cut indicolite tourmaline from Minas Gerais, Brazil. From the W. Larson collection. Photo by Harold and Erica Van Pelt.

also has an 880-carat kunzite, and the Royal Ontario Museum possesses an 1,800-carat greenish yellow spodumene.

One of the most famous Brazilian gemstones is an 1,847-carat aquamarine that was presented to President Franklin D. Roosevelt by the Brazilian government. This extraordinary aquamarine, possibly the world's largest, is now housed in the Roosevelt Museum in Hyde Park, New York.

The Natural History Museum of Los Angeles County also has several important faceted Brazilian gemstones. Among the most notable are a 638-carat aquamarine, a 461.4-carat morganite, a 286-carat green beryl, and a 211.5-carat cat's-eye golden beryl. It also has what is perhaps the world's largest kunzite, a 1,267-carat stone found in the 1960s.

Recently, very large blue topazes have been faceted that overshadow anything previously recorded for size in Brazilian gemstones. The Natural History Museum of Los Angeles County's 5,350-carat stone, once a record weight, appears insignificant in size next to the American Museum of Natural History's 21,005-carat "Brazilian Princess" and the 22,892-carat yellow topaz in the Smithsonian collection.

Figure 4-14. Gem kunzite crystal from Minas Gerais, Brazil. Photo by Harold and Erica Van Pelt.

Figure 4-15. *This extraordinary necklace from the A. Blythe collection exhibits the best variety of colors that tourmaline may possess. While much of the world's finest tourmaline is from the pegmatites of Minas Gerais, Brazil, other fine tourmalines may be found in parts of Africa, southern California, and Afghanistan. Photo by Harold and Erica Van Pelt.*

REFERENCES

Atkinson, D., and R. Z. Kothavala. 1983. Kashmir sapphire. *Gems & Gemology* 19(2):64–76.

Bariand, P., and J. F. Poullen. 1978. The pegmatites of Laghman, Nuristan, Afghanistan. *Mineralogical Record* 9(5):301–308.

Bowersox, G. W. 1985. A status report on gemstones from Afghanistan. *Gems & Gemology* 21(4):192–204.

Cameron, E. N., R. H. Jahns, A. M. McNair, and L. R. Page. 1949. *Internal Structure of Granitic Pegmatites.* Monograph 2. Economic Geology, Urbana, Ill.

Cassedanne, J. P., and J. Lowell. 1982. Famous mineral localities: The Virgem da Lapa pegmatites. *Mineralogical Record* 18(1):19–28.

Cassedanne, J. P., and D. A. Sauer. 1980. Famous mineral localities: The Cruzeiro mine past and present. *Mineralogical Record* 11(6):363–370.

Cerny, P., ed. 1982. *Granitic Pegmatites in Science and Industry.* Short Course Handbook 8. Mineralogical Association of Canada, Winnipeg.

Da Costa, M. T., and A. Romano. 1976. *Mapa geologico do Estado de Minas Gerais.* Secr. Plan. & Coord. geral. Inst. Geoc. apl., Belo Horizonte.

Dirac, F., and H. Ebert. 1967. Isotopic age from the pegmatite provinces of Eastern Brazil. *Nature* 215:948–949.

Fersman, A. E. 1931. *Les Pegmatites, leur Importance Scientifique et Practique.* Akademiya Nauk, SSSR, Leningrad. (Translated from Russian into French under the direction of R. du Tricu de Terdonck and J. Thoreau, Universite de Louvain, Louvain, Belgium, 1952.)

Ginzburg, A. I., I. N. Timofeyev, and L. G. Feldman. 1979. *Principles of Geology of Granitic Pegmatites (in Russia).* Nedra, Moscow. (Summarized in Cerny, 1982).

Heinrich, E. W. 1956. Radioactive pegmatite deposits: How to know them. *Canadian Mining Journal* 77(4):69–72, 100.

Hutchinson, R. W., and R. J. Claus. 1956. Pegmatite deposits, Alto, Ligauha, Portuguese East Africa. *Econ. Geol.* 51:757–780.

Jahns, R. H. 1953. The genesis of pegmatites. I. Occurrence and origin of giant crystals. *American Mineralogist* 38:563–598.

Jahns, R. H. 1954. Pegmatites of Southern California. *California Div. Mines and Geology Bull.* 170 (C7-P5):37–50.

Jahns, R. H. 1955. The study of pegmatites. *Econ. Geol.* 50:1025–1130.

Jahns, R. H. 1979. Gem-bearing pegmatites in San Diego

County, 1–38. In P. L. Abbott and V. R. Todd, eds., *Mesozoic Crystalline Rocks: Peninsular Ranges Batholith and Pegmatites, Point Sal Ophiolite.* Department of Geological Sciences, San Diego State University, San Diego.

Jahns, R. H., and C. W. Burnham. 1969. Experimental studies of pegmatite genesis. I. A model for the derivation and crystallization of granitic pegmatites. *Econ. Geol.* 64:843–864.

Jahns, R. H., and L. A. Wright. 1951. *Gem- and Lithium-Bearing Pegmatites of the Pala District, San Diego County, California.* California Div. Mines Spec. Rept. 7-A, Sacramento, 72 pages.

Middlemiss, C. S. 1931. *Precious and Semi-Precious Gemstones of Jammu and Kashmir.* Jammu and Kashmir Mineral Survey Reports 9, Jammu. 58 pages.

Murdock, T. G. 1963. *Mineral Resources of the Malagasy Republic.* U.S. Bureau of Mines Information Circular 8196. 147 pages.

Neiva, J., and J. Neves. 1960. Pegmatites of Alto-Ligonha, Mozambique. *Int. Geol. Cong. Proc.* (21st, Copenhagen) 17:53–62.

Page, L. R., J. W. Adams, M. P. Erickson, W. E. Hall, J. B. Hanley, P. Joralemon, J. J. Norton, L. C. Pray, T. A. Steven, W. C. Stoll, and R. F. Stopper. 1953. *Pegmatite Investigations, 1942–1945, Black Hills, South Dakota.* USGS Prof. Paper 247, Washington, D.C.

Pecora, W. T., M. R. Klepper, and D. M. Larrabec. 1950a. *Mica Deposits in Minas Gerais, Brazil.* USGS Bull. 964-c., Washington, D.C., 305 pages.

Pecora, W. T., G. Switzer, A. L. de My Barbosa, and A. T. Myers, 1950b. Structure and mineralogy of the Col conda pegmatite, Minas Gerais, Brazil. *American Mineralogist* 35 (9/10):889–901.

Proctor, K. 1984. Gem pegmatites of Minas Gerais, Brazil: Exploration, occurrence and aquamarine deposits. *Gems & Gemology* 20(2):78–100.

Proctor, K 1985. Gem pegmatites of Minas Gerais, Brazil: The tourmalines of the Aracual districts. *Gems & Gemology* 2(1):3–19.

Proctor, K. 1985b. Gem pegmatites of Minas Gerais, Brazil: The tourmaline of the Governador Valadares District. *Gems & Gemology* 21(2):86–104.

Schneiderhohn, H. 1961. *Die Erzlagerstatten der Erde,* vol. 2. *Die Pegmatite.* Gustav Fischer Verlag, Stuttgart. 720 pages.

Shigley, J. E., and A. R. Kampf. 1984. Gem-bearing pegmatites: A review. *Gems & Gemology* 20(2): 64–77.

Sinkankas, J. 1981. *Emeralds and Other Beryls.* Chilton Book Company, Radnor, Pa. 665 pages.

Solesbury, F. W. 1967. Gem Corundum Pegmatites in N.E. Tanganyika. *Econ. Geol.* 62:983–991.

5

Gemstones Formed Directly from Molten Rock:
The Ruby Deposits of Chanthaburi-Trat, Thailand

Molten lava erupting from fissures or volcanoes on the earth's surface may be a source for gemstones. These hot lavas may contain gems in one of three ways: (1) Gemstones such as moonstone may be an essential constituent of the lava and crystallize as such as the lava cools; (2) in the final stages of cooling, when much of the magma has solidified, minerals such as topaz may crystallize in lithophysal (gas) cavities formed in the cooling lava; and (3) the lava may simply act as the vehicle that transports materials that crystallized at great depth to the surface. Such is the case with many alkali-olivine basalts, which may bring peridot, zircon, sapphire, or ruby up from 100-km depths (Fig. 5-1).

Moonstone is a variety of the potassium-rich feldspar, orthoclase, and its high-temperature polymorph, sanidine. It is distinguished by its display of a silver-blue sheen known as *adulerescence*. Orthoclase is a common constituent of granitic pegmatites, and sanidine is common in the higher-temperature rhyolitic lavas. Moonstone is found in all of these environments, although rarely in sizes and qualities suitable for use as a gemstone.

Sri Lanka is by far the most important source of moonstone. In Sri Lanka, the moonstone occurs in feldspar-rich dikes near Ambalangoda in the Southern Province and in the Kandy district in the Central Province. Characteristically reddish brown moonstone occurs in the Coimbatore district of Madras, India (Webster, 1975).

Moonstone is also found in numerous localities in the United States. It is generally believed that the finest are found in the interior of large, chalky white crystals associated in granitic dikes on the west slope of the Black Range in Grant County, New Mexico (Sinkankas, 1959).

Topaz is typically found in gem-bearing granitic pegmatites, in hydrothermal veins, and in lithophysal cavities in rhyolite. Topaz as a late-stage lithophysal cavity filling is best known from the

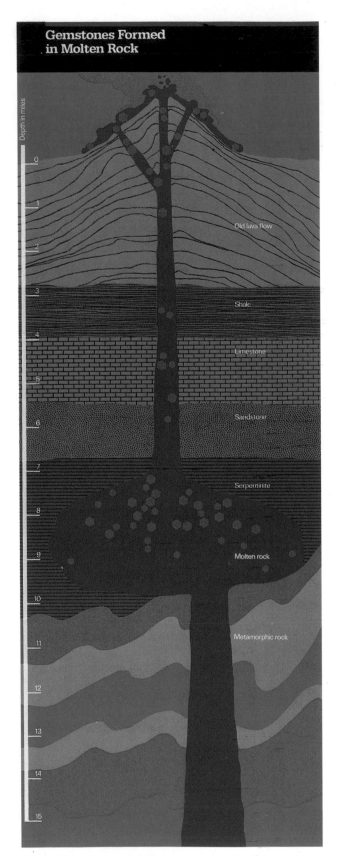

Gemstones Formed in Molten Rock

Depth in miles

0
1
2
3
4
5
6
7
8
9
10
11
12
13
14
15

Old lava flow

Shale

Limestone

Sandstone

Serpentinite

Molten rock

Metamorphic rock

Figure 5-1. Diagram showing processes leading to the magmatic occurrence of rubies. Courtesy of the Natural History Museum of Los Angeles County.

topaz-bearing rhyolites in the southern end of the Thomas Mountains in Juab County, Utah (Sinkankas, 1959).

A similar topaz occurrence is found in San Luis Potosí, Mexico. Unfortunately, these topaz crystals as well as the similar ones from Utah tend to fade to colorlessness when exposed to light for prolonged periods of time.

Rare, red beryl has recently been commercially produced from similar lithophysal cavities in rhyolite in the Wah Wah mountains of southwestern Utah. These unique beryls are believed to have formed from a gas or vapor phase given off by a rhyolitic magma as it was cooling (Shigley and Foord, 1984), and the intense red color of these unique beryls seems to be caused by trace amounts of manganese.

From a gemologist's point of view, the materials brought up as passengers in the voluminous alkali basalts found around the world are the most interesting. These basalts, sometimes known as *flood basalts* because they appear to be so widespread, may bring with them nodules containing zircon, ruby, and/or sapphire or volcanic "bombs" of olivine (peridot) that are thought to represent broken fragments of the Earth's upper mantle.

One of the best examples of an upper mantle material, olivine (peridot), being transported tens of kilometers to the earth's surface is an alkali basalt found on Peridot Mesa near San Carlos, Arizona. Here, elliptical to angular bombs of olivine (peridot) up to 20 cm in diameter make up 25 to 40 percent of the rock volume (Broomfield and Shride, 1956; Holloway and Cross, 1978; Vuich and Moore, 1977). The roughly 3-square-km Mesa itself is capped by the basalt, which is 10 to 100 feet thick and was believed to have been erupted from a volcanic core that occupies the southwest corner of Peridot Mesa. The olivine bombs are mostly granular, but contain irregular fragments of peridot up to 2 cm in diameter. These fragments are mined by the local Apache Indians and currently represent a very high percentage of the peridot supplied to the world's gem market (Koivula, 1981). Mineralogically similar nodules are commonly characteristic of alkali basalts, but included fragments of gem peridot are considered quite rare. Recently, a similar occurrence with tremendous gem potential was reported from the Tertiary age Hanluoba basalt in the Xuanhua area of Hebei Province, China (Keller and Wang, 1986).

Other than peridot, a principal constituent of the earth's mantle, relatively few gemstones are thought to be formed at great depth and transported to the surface as xenocrystic passengers in alkali basalts. However, ruby and/or sapphire and zircon occur in such an environment and typically are found together as a suite, although they are also found individually. At Yogo Gulch, Montana, where fine cornflower blue sapphires occur in a gabbroic dike 2 to 7 m wide (Clabaugh, 1952), no zircons or rubies are present, although some of the pink Yogo sapphires approach ruby in color. More typical, however, are the sapphire and zircon facilities on Hainan Island and at Mingsi in Fujian Province, China (Keller and Keller, 1986), which have not yet been fully developed. The sapphires and zircons are found eluvially in what was a deeply weathered alkali basalt. Very similar deposits have recently been discovered in the Mercaderes–Río Mayo area in the state of Cauca, Colombia (Keller et al., 1985).

The geologic situation is almost identical to the gem fields at Anakie, Queensland, and in the New England district of New South Wales, Australia (Coldham, 1985). The New England district centers on the towns of Inverell and Glen Innes. Due to the production of Anakie and New England, Australia is currently the supplier of between 50 and 70 percent of the world's sapphires. Both areas produce abundant yellow and dark blue-green sapphires, along with pale yellow to brown zircons. The gemstones are all recovered from alluvial and eluvial deposits derived from deeply weathered alkali basalts (MacNevin, 1971). The gemstones are associated with black spinel (pleonaste) and are thought originally to have been constituents of xenocrysts brought up from great depths. The alkali basalt acted, as in many other areas of the world, as an elevator for the gemstones that moved them up to the surface where they spilled out as constituents of widespread lava flows that quickly weathered to an iron-rich (lateritic) soil (Thompson, 1983).

The classic occurrence of gems coming from depth is found in the alkali basalt fields extending across Indochina. In Indochina, the occurrence of gems varies regularly from east to west in very similar alkali basalt flows across the peninsula. In Vietnam, the eastern extension of the flows, only zircon has been recovered, the best examples being found in the Kha district (Webster, 1975). Zircon occurrences continue westward into eastern and north-central Kampuchea. The occurrence of gem-quality zircon has been described from the Ratanakiri Quaternary basaltic maslif in northern Kampuchea by Lacombe (1970). In western Kampuchea, however, zircon diminishes in importance, and sapphire becomes dominant along with ruby at the famous Pailin deposits (Berrange and Jobbins, 1976). These deposits are almost continuous westward into Thailand, where the Chanthaburi-Trat area produces huge quantities of gem ruby from deeply weathered alkali basalta, and zircon and sapphire diminish in importance. Further west, ruby gives way to sapphire in the Kanchanaburi area west of Bangkok. Today, the Chanthaburi-Trat gem field is of greatest importance.

The Chanthaburi-Trat Gem Field, Thailand

Thailand has been a world supplier of gem ruby and sapphire since the latter part of the nineteenth century, although the deposits were not thought to be as important as those of neighboring Burma. In 1963, however, the Burmese deposits were nationalized, and supplies of fine gems from these mines declined rapidly. The fact that so little is produced in Burma today has catapulted the Thai deposits into importance. An estimated 70 percent of the world's high-quality gem rubies now come from Thailand. Of these, 85 to 90 percent come from the Chanthaburi-Trat district alone (Aranyakanon and Vichit, 1979). Although the overall quality of these rubies is not as high as those found in Burma, some stones are exceptional (Fig. 5-2).

The gem deposits of the Chanthaburi-Trat (formerly Krat) area are entirely alluvial, having eroded out of deeply weathered basalt flows (Fig. 5-3). The region can be divided into two mining districts based on the type of corundum produced. The first lies to the west, near the town of Chanthaburi and in the Chanthaburi province. It includes the famous Khao Ploi Waen and Bang Kha Cha mining areas, known for their production of blue, blue-green, and yellow sapphires, as well as black star sapphires. The second district, approximately 45

Figure 5-2. Two fine Thai rubies weighing 3.41 and 3.04 carats. Photo courtesy of Jack S. D. Abraham, Precious Gem Resources, Inc., New York.

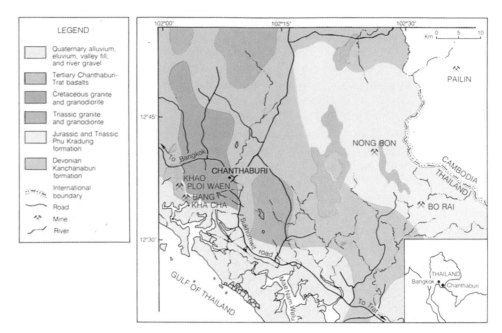

Figure 5-3. Geologic sketchmap of the Chanthaburi-Trat area's major ruby and sapphire mines. Modified from Vichit and associates (1978) and Javanaphet (1969). Courtesy of the Gemological Institute of America.

km to the east of Chanthaburi, in Trat province, is the currently very active Bo Rai/Bo Waen mining area, known for its significant production of ruby. In fact, Bo Rai/Bo Waen, together with the Pailin area 27 km to the northeast in Kampuchea (formerly Cambodia), comprises the most important ruby-producing area in the world today (Fig. 5-4). Occasionally, green sapphires and color-change sapphires occur in this district as well.

In 1980, an estimated 39.4 million carats of ruby and sapphire were mined in the Chanthaburi-Trat area by an estimated workforce of 20,000 miners; these figures have more than doubled since 1973 (Stamm, 1981). Translating this production figure into official export figures is difficult because the latter does not include smuggled material or tourist purchases that do not have to be declared at customs. In addition, the tremendous amount of corundum from elsewhere, particularly Sri Lanka and Australia, that is brought to Thailand for heat treatment and then sold in the gem markets of Bangkok undoubtedly has a major effect on any export statistics. The actual production and export figures are probably much greater than those estimated by the Department of Customs and the Department of Business Economics.

Considering the importance of the Thai deposits, surprisingly little has been written about them. Bauer and Spencer (1904) provide one of the best early descriptions and a detailed map of the deposits. Most of the more recent work done by the Geological Survey of Thailand has been published in Thai journals which are, for the most part, difficult to obtain in the United States. An excellent

Figure 5-4. Independent miners often work the tailings of the more sophisticated operations in hopes of recovering any overlooked ruby. This photo was taken at Bo Rai by Peter C. Keller.

general study of the gem deposits of Thailand was done by Aranyakanon and Vichit (1979). This report included details on the Chanthaburi-Trat area. Charaljavanaphet (1951) did one of the earliest geological reports on the Bo Rai area. One of the most important geological studies of the corundum-related basalts in Thailand was by Vichit and associates (1978). Berrange and Jobbins (1976) did a superbly detailed study of the gem deposits at Pailin, Cambodia, in which they included many references to the deposits in the Chanthaburi-Trat area. A summary of this work was recently published by Jobbins and Berrange (1981). Articles by visitors to the area include Moreau (1976), Chang (1969), Pavitt (1973), and Keller (1982).

Location and Access

The Chanthaburi-Trat mining district is located in southeastern Thailand, approximately 330 km east-southeast of the capital city of Bangkok. The district extends from approximately 102° to 103° west longitude and 12° to 13° north latitude. The district is contiguous with the very productive Pailin ruby and sapphire gem field, 27 km northeast of Bo Rai in Kampuchea.

Access to Chanthaburi is quite easy now compared to the late nineteenth century, when, according to Bauer and Spencer (1904), a 20-hour journey by steamer from Bangkok was required. A new highway has shortened the trip from Bangkok to Chanthaburi to 3 hours. Bo Rai is an additional 45 km from Chanthaburi eastward via highway 3157. Currently, there are more than 20 active operations, varying from hand to highly mechanized.

History

Gem mining in the Chanthaburi-Trat area was first reported at Khao Ploi Waen, also known as Pagoda Hill and Hill of Gems, in 1850. Khao Ploi Waen is about 8 km southwest of Chanthaburi, near the village of Bang Kha Cha. In 1850, the Shans and Burmese were mining sapphires here (Pavitt, 1973). According to Bauer and Spencer (1904), a missionary report dated 1859 stated that a handful of rubies could be collected from the Hill of Gems in half an hour. Interestingly, the pagoda that Bauer and Spencer cites still stands.

Bauer and Spencer (1904) described the state of the ruby and sapphire deposits in the Trat province (then known as Krat) in the 1870s and 1880s. He divided the district into two groups roughly 50 km apart: Bo Nawang, an area of about 40 square kilometers; and Bo Channa, 50 km to the northeast and a little over a square km in extent. Bauer noted

that the mines at Bo Nawang were typically small pits a meter deep sunk in coarse yellow-brown sand overlying a bed of clay. The rubies occurred at the base of the sand unit in a layer 15 to 25 cm thick. These mines have been worked since about 1875.

In 1895, an English company, The Sapphires and Rubies of Siam, Ltd., obtained the rights to mine in what was then Siam. This company was an extension of E. W. Streeter, a famous London jeweler with a Burmese gem-mining operation known as Burma Ruby Mines Ltd. The company was not successful in the Chanthaburi-Trat area (Bauer and Spencer, 1904).

At Bo Channa, which has been worked since about 1885, the mines were vertical shafts extending to a depth of 7 to 8 m until they reached a gem gravel 15 to 60 cm thick. Bauer and Spencer estimated that about 1,250 Burmese miners worked the Bo Channa and Bo Nawang areas at the time.

Since the introduction of the Siam Mining Act in 1919, all gem mining has been limited to Thai nationals. Today, about 2,000 people mine in the Khao Ploi Waen–Bang Kha Cha area, and at least 20,000 people work between Bo Rai, Bo Waen, Nong Bon, and the deposits at Pailin in Kampuchea. Interviews at Bo Rai revealed that at least 1,000 miners from the area cross into Kampuchea every day.

Geology

Because of the deep chemical weathering and subsequent rapid erosion that is typically associated with tropical climates, the corundum deposits of the Chanthaburi-Trat district occur exclusively in alluvial, eluvial, or residual lateritic soil deposits derived from underlying basalt flows. The gems have long been thought to have been derived from these basalts, although reports of in situ occurrences are rare (Vichit et al., 1978).

Although the precise age of the basalts has not yet been determined, they are thought to be relatively young; estimates range from Tertiary to Pleistocene (Leon Silver, personal communication, 1982). According to Jobbins and Berrange (1981), the closely related Pailin basalts have been radiometrically determined to be 1.4 to 2.14 million years old. This places the basalts in Upper Pliocene to Lower Pleistocene age. They have been informally designated the Chanthaburi-Trat basalts by Vichit et al. (1978). These flows unconformably overlie the Devonian-age O Smoet formation and Triassic-age Tadeth group that Berrange and Jobbins (1976) discuss in their comprehensive study of the Pailin gem field. Other noteworthy geologic units in the region include granites and granodiorites of possible Cretaceous age and the Triassic-age Khao Sa-Bab granite that outcrops just east of Chanthaburi (Javanaphet, 1969).

Outcrops of the Chanthaburi-Trat basalt are rare. The only notable outcrops are at Khao Ploi Waen and Khao Wao. At Khao Ploi Waen, it occurs as a dark, fine-grained to glassy vesicular basalt; the hill itself is thought to be a volcanic plug that is possibly a source for the gem-bearing basalt flows in the area (Taylor and Buravas, 1951). The plug at Khao Ploi Waen yields blue, green, and yellow sapphires as well as black star sapphires. Rubies are rare at this locality.

Invariably, the gem deposits are associated with basalt flows or at least remnant flows. The flow at Chanthaburi is only about 35 square kilometers, but the basalts in the Bo Rai area are much more extensive. As expected, the basalt flows parallel to the gem deposits, trending in a north-south direction. The flow in the Bo Rai area, about 27 km by 4 km, roughly delineates the Bo Rai mining district, which Vichit and associates (1978) estimate to consist of about 23 gem localities. Bo Rai produces ruby almost exclusively.

From a petrographic point of view, the Chanthaburi-Trat basalts are fine-grained, olivine-bearing alkaline basalts called *basanitoids* by Vichit et al. (1978) and *basanites* by Berrange and Jobbins (1976). These basalts locally contain spinel-rich lherzolite nodules, which may, in fact, be the ultimate source for the corundum. Lherzolite nodules are thought to form in the upper mantle of the earth, at depths of about 50 km, and may be unrelated to the magmas that brought them to the surface. The basalts contain augite, pyrope garnet, calcic plagioclase, zircon, spinel, and magnetite. The magnetite has been reported as megacrysts up to 6 cm in diameter. Spinel, which along with olivine and enstatite is typical of lherzolite, is locally abundant but rarely of gem quality.

The structural and historical geology of the Chanthaburi-Trat area is essentially identical to that outlined by Jobbins and Berrange (1981) for the Pailin area of Kampuchea, which could easily be considered part of the Chanthaburi-Trat district. Jobbins and Berrange note that during the Himalayan orogeny of early to middle Tertiary times, the region, which is largely underlain by Jurassic-Triassic sandstones and Devonian phyllites, was uplifted and intruded by granites and granodiorites as represented by the Khao Sa-Bob granite. During the final stages of this orogenic episode, the area was also intruded by basaltic dikes that spilled onto the earth's surface in the form of extensive basaltic lava flows. Some volcanic features, such as the volcanic plug now exposed as a remnant at Khao Ploi Waen, were also formed at this time. Since this period of mountain building and volcanic activity, the area has been geologically quiet, and the surface has been exposed to intense weathering and erosion as a consequence of the harsh tropical climate. Deep residual soil horizons formed over the basalts, which locally have been eroded and redeposited to form the secondary gem deposits of the region. Because corundum is durable and heavy, it is an ideal mineral for concentration in these alluvial or eluvial deposits.

The gem deposits in the Chanthaburi-Trat area vary greatly in thickness, depending on the topography of the area and the bedrock. In the Chanthaburi area, sapphires are found on the surface at the Khao Ploi Waen and at a depth of 3 to 8 m in the area adjoining the hill and at Bang Kha Cha. In the relatively flat Bo Rai area, the gem gravel is at a depth of at least 4 to 10 m and varies in thickness from 0.3 m to 1 m. At Bo Rai, the ruby is associated with black spinel, olivine, and, in rare instances, blue, green, or color-change sapphires.

Mining Methods

The methods used to mine ruby and sapphire in the Chanthaburi area reflect all levels of technological sophistication, from the simple rattan basket to the most advanced bulldozer. The mining in the Khao Ploi Waen area is typical of Thailand's most primitive extraction methods. Independent miners lease land from the local owners. They dig a vertical shaft about 1 m in diameter to a depth of about 10 m, where the gem gravels are usually intersected. No ladder is used; miners simply dig footholes into the side of the shaft. The soil is lifted to the surface with a large bamboo crane and rattan baskets. When the gem gravels are encountered, they are washed in artificial pools and sorted by hand in round rattan sieves. According to Pavitt (1973), about 2,000 people work using these simple methods in the Khao Ploi Waen area alone.

Just to the south of Khao Ploi Waen, at Bang Kha Cha, which is famous for its black star sapphires and blue and green sapphires, a different style of mining can be seen. Here, the sapphires are recovered from the muddy tidal flats of the Gulf of Siam, which is located about 5 km to the south. The gem miners take boats out into the flats at low tide and fill them with the gem-bearing mud. They then take the mud to shore, where it is washed with the standard rattan sieves. More sophisticated operations are conducted at Bang Kha Cha, but the most technologically advanced mining can be seen at Bo Rai, the ruby mines located on the border of Kampuchea, where claims are generally about 1,620 m square and the landscape is dotted with bulldozers and sophisticated washing equipment.

Large-scale mechanized mining was formally banned in Thailand in 1980 in response to pressure from farmers who claimed that the mining was destroying the topsoil. Even so, the majority of the ruby-mining operations observed during my recent visit to Bo Rai used bulldozers to remove the overburden and high-pressure water cannons to wash the gem gravel that is then pumped into sluices from which the ruby is recovered (Fig. 5-5). According to Stamm (1981), "special" permits that allow mechanized mining are issued for 2,500 baht ($125) per month. In addition to the bulldozers and water cannons, the latest mechanical treatment includes a jig or willoughby table washer to concentrate the corundum at the end of the long sluice (Figs. 5-6 and 5-7). Most of these so-called new mining methods at Bo Rai have been borrowed from the basic principles of alluvial tin mining used at Phuket, on the southern extension of Thailand.

Not all ruby mining in the Bo Rai area is mechanized; here, too, some is done by pit miners using only the traditional rattan sieve (Fig. 5-8). These pit miners may work in small groups or on a few square meters of leased land (Figs. 5-9, 5-10, and 5-11). Many of them are refugees from nearby Kampuchea. They commonly pay the government or landowner about 500 baht ($25) per month and are

Figure 5-5. At Bo Rai, gem gravels are washed by high-pressure water cannons and transported up a pipe (seen to the right in photo) to a long sluice. Photo by Peter C. Keller.

permitted to keep what they recover. Other small mining groups search the already worked tailings of the large, mechanized operations. Usually these small miners are successful enough to support themselves and their families. Commonly, miners can be observed sorting and selling their ruby production in front of their homes.

Characteristics of Thai Ruby and Sapphire

The rubies taken from the basalt fields of southeastern Thailand can generally be distinguished by their color (Fig. 5-12) and unique inclusions from those derived from the crystalline limestone terrain of Burma or from the graphite gneisses of East Africa. Gübelin's (1940, 1971) detailed studies of inclusions typical of Thai rubies indicate that the most common inclusions are subhexagonal to rounded opaque metallic grains of pyrrhotite, $Fe_{1-x}S$; yellowish hexagonal platelets of apatite, $Ca_5(PO_4)_3(OH,F,Cl)$; and reddish brown almandite garnets, $Fe_3Al_2(SiO_4)_3$. These inclusions were commonly surrounded by circular feathers and characteristic polysynthetic twinning planes.

A parcel of more than 500 rough rubies I obtained from mines in the Bo Rai area were examined for characteristic inclusions and any other distinguishing features. The parcel consisted of well-rounded fragments, generally under 5 mm, that exhibited color variations from strongly violet to a classic pigeon blood red. Grains larger than a centimeter were rare. The refractive index (1.766–1.774) and specific gravity (3.97–4.05) of ruby do not differ with locality. The high iron content of the Thai rubies does influence their behavior when exposed to ultraviolet radiation in that their fluorescence is inhibited significantly; the parcel examined exhibited the very weak fluorescence expected for Thai rubies.

By far the most common inclusion in the parcel of rubies studied was subhedral to anhedral pyrrhotite, which was commonly altered to a black submetallic material that x-ray diffraction analysis by Chuck Fryer of GIA revealed to be goethite, FeO(OH). Because basalts are unusually high in iron, pyrrhotite inclusions in rubies from a basaltic terrain are not surprising. Furthermore, according to Carmichael and associates (1974), pyrrhotite appears to be the dominant primary sulfide in basaltic rocks.

In all the samples studied, no inclusions of almandite garnet or rutile were observed, and yellowish anhedral hexagonal platelets of translucent apatite were rarely noted. A high percentage of the stones studied were totally free of diagnostic min-

Figure 5-6. After the gem gravels exit the pipe, they are run over a long sluice. The heavier corundum concentrate collects in a jig at the end. Photo by Peter C. Keller.

Figure 5-7. A jig or willoughby table washer, a device borrowed from the Phuket tin mines on the southern extension of Thailand, is very effective at concentrating ruby. Photo by Peter C. Keller.

Figure 5-8. Primitive washing of gem gravels at Chanthaburi-Trat area. Photo by Peter C. Keller.

Figure 5-9. Hand pumps assist the independent miners in controlling the flooding of their workings. Photo by Peter C. Keller.

Figure 5-10. Many of the independent miners at Bo Rai are Kampuchean refugees, as suggested by their dress. Photo by Peter C. Keller.

Figure 5-11. The independent miners at Bo Rai use brass trays to sort their rubies. Photo by Peter C. Keller.

Figure 5-12. *Over 70 percent of the world's ruby comes from the area near Chanthaburi on the Thai-Cambodian border. This extraordinary ruby and diamond necklace from the Brent Laird collection is a superb example of the Thai ruby. Photo by Harold and Erica Van Pelt.*

eral inclusions, however; the most characteristic features in these stones were secondary stains of iron oxide that appeared in almost all fractures. Given the iron-rich nature of the presumed host basalt, this abundance of iron is to be expected. The brownish to purplish overtones of the rubies and their weak fluorescence when exposed to shortwave ultraviolet and x-radiation has been attributed to the characteristically high concentrations of iron found in the Thai rubies.

Sapphires recovered from the Khao Ploi Waen and Bang Kha Cha areas outside of Chanthaburi are quite different morphologically from the formless Bo Rai rubies. These sapphires show signs of transport, in that they occur as well-rounded hexagonal prisms. I would suggest, however, that the sapphires have not traveled as far as the rubies, which rarely exhibit any of their original hexagonal morphology. The sapphires are generally green, blue, yellow, or black, and the black sapphires commonly exhibit asterism. They range in diameter from less than a millimeter to 10 cm, with an average size of 3 to 6 mm. Large, hexagonal blue-green sapphire specimens as large as 1,720 carats have been reported from the Bang Kha Cha area (Pavitt, 1973), but no gem-quality stones of this size have ever been reported.

REFERENCES

Aranyakanon, P., and P. Vichit. 1979. *Gemstones in Thailand.* Unpublished report for the Economic Geology Division of the Ministry of Industry of Thailand.

Bauer, M., and L. J. Spencer. 1904. *Precious Stones* (trans. of 1896 German text). Charles Griffin & Co., London. 647 pages.

Berrange, J. P., and E. A. Jobbins. 1976. *The Geology, Gemmology, Mining Methods and Economic Potential of the Pailin Ruby and Sapphire Gem-field, Khmer Republic.* Institute of Geological Sciences Report 35, London. 32 pages.

Broomfield, C. S., and A. R. Shride. 1956. Mineral resources of the San Carlos Indian Reservation, Arizona. *U.S. Geol. Surv. Bull.* 1027-n:613–691.

Carmichael, I., F. Turner, and J. Verhoogen. 1974. *Igneous Petrology.* McGraw-Hill Book Co., New York.

Chang, F. 1969. A trip to Chanthaburi, Thailand. *Lapidary Journal* 23:1020–1024.

Charaljavanaphet, J. 1951. Gem deposits at Bo Na-Wong, Tok-Phrom, Bo-Rai in Chanthaburi and Trat provinces. *Geologic Reconnaissance of the Mineral Deposits of Thailand: Geological Survey Memoir* 1:148–150.

Clabaugh, S. E. 1952. Corundum Deposits of Montana. *U.S. Geol. Surv. Bull.* 983.

Coldham, T. 1985. Sapphires from Australia. *Gems & Gemology* 21(3):130–146.

Gübelin, E. 1940. Differences between Burmese and Siamese rubies. *Gems & Gemology* 3:69–72.

Gübelin, E. 1971. New analytical results of the inclusions in Siam rubies. *Journal of Australian Gemmology* 12(7):242–252.

Holloway, J. R., and C. Cross. 1978. The San Carlos Alkaline Rock Association. *Arizona Bur. Geol. Min. Tech. Spec. Pap.* 2:171–173.

Javanaphet, J. C. 1969. *Geological Map of Thailand 1:1,000,000.* Department of Mineral Resources, Bangkok.

Jobbins, E. A., and J. P. Berrange. 1981. The Pailin ruby and sapphire gemfield, Cambodia. *Journal of Gemology* 17(8):555–567.

Keller, A., and P. Keller. 1986. The sapphires of Mingxi, Fujian Province, China. *Gems and Gemology* 22:41–45.

Keller, P. C. 1982. The Chanthaburi-Trat gem field, Thailand. *Gems & Gemology* 18(4):186–196.

Keller, P. C., J. I. Koivula, and G. Jara. 1985. Sapphire from the Mercaderes–Rio Mayo area, Cauca, Columbia. *Gems & Gemology* 21(1):20–25.

Keller, P. C., and F. Wang. 1986. A survey of the gemstone resources of China. *Gems & Gemology* 22:3–13.

Koivula, J. 1981. San Carlos peridot. *Gems & Gemology* 17:205–214.

Lacombe, P. 1970. Le massif basaltique quaternaire a zircons-gemmes de Ratanakiri, Cambodge nord-oriental. *French Bur. Recherches Geol. et Minieres Bull.* (ser. 2) 4(2):29–53; (4)33–71.

MacNevin, A. A. 1971. Sources of sapphires in the New England District, New South Wales. *New South Wales Geol. Surv. Quart. Notes* 3:1–5

Moreau, M. 1976. Nong Bon ou le rubis de thailande. *Revue de Gemmologie a.f.g.* 47:10–12.

Pavitt, J. A. L. 1973. Sapphire mining in Chanthaburi (Thailand). *Journal of Gemmology* 13:302–307.

Shigley, J. E. and E. E. Foord. 1984. Gem-quality red beryl from the Wah Wah Mountains, Utah. *Gems & Gemology* 20(4):208–221.

Sinkankas, J. 1959. *Gemstones of North America.* Van Nostrand Reinhold Company, New York.

Stamm, D. 1981. A star is born: New facets of Thailand's gem trade. *New Look Investor* 13(8):8–20.

Taylor, G. C., and S. Buravas. 1951. Gem deposits at Khao Ploi Waen and Bang Ka Cha, Chanthaburi Province. Geologic Reconnaissance of the mineral deposits of Thailand. *Geological Survey Memoir* 1:144–148.

Thompson, D. 1983. *Sapphires in New South Wales.* Dept. of Mineral Resources, New South Wales, Sydney, Australia.

Vichit, P., S. Vudhichativanich, and R. Hansawek. 1978. The distribution and some characteristics of corundum-bearing basalts in Thailand. *Journal of the Geological Society of Thailand* 3:M4-1–M4-38.

Vuich, J., and R. Moore. 1977. Bureau studies olivine resources on San Carlos Apache Reservation. *Arizona Bur. Mines Field Notes* 7(2):6–10.

Webster, R. 1975. *Gems: Their Sources, Descriptions and Identification.* Butterworths, London. 938 pages.

PART III

Gemstones Formed by Very High Temperatures and Pressures

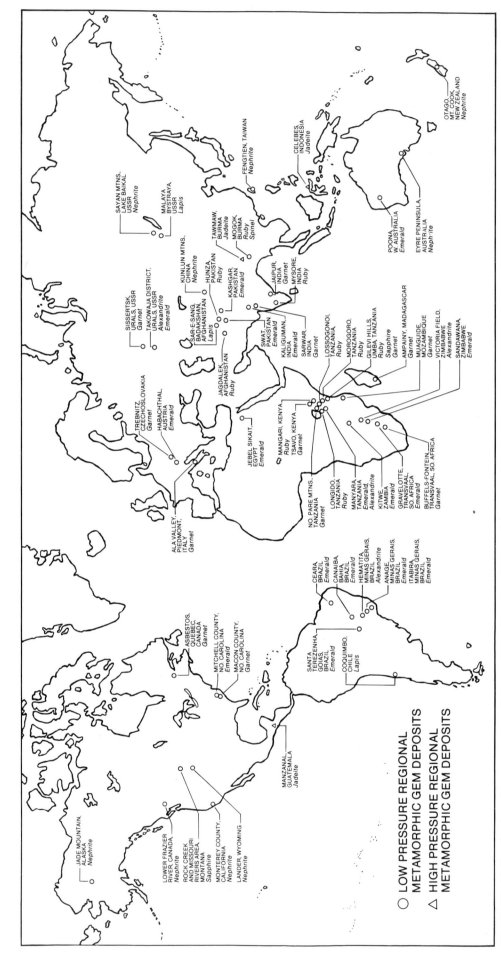

Map 3. *World distribution of important gem deposits formed by great heat and pressure.*

JADE MOUNTAIN,
ALASKA
Nephrite

LOWER FRAZIER
RIVER, CANADA
Nephrite

ROCK CREEK
AND MISSOURI
RIVERS AREA,
MONTANA
Sapphire

MONTEREY COUNTY,
CALIFORNIA
Nephrite

LANDER, WYOMING
Nephrite

ASBESTOS,
QUEBEC,
CANADA
Garnet

MITCHELL COUNTY,
NO. CAROLINA
Emerald

MACON COUNTY,
NO. CAROLINA
Garnet

MANZANAL,
GUATEMALA
Jadeite

SANTA
TEREZENHA,
GOIAS,
BRAZIL
Emerald

COQUIMBO,
CHILE
Lapis

CEARA,
BRAZIL
Emerald

CANAIBA,
BAHIA,
BRAZIL
Emerald

HEMATITA,
MINAS GERAIS,
BRAZIL
Alexandrite

ANAGE,
MINAS GERAIS,
BRAZIL
Emerald

ITABIRA,
MINAS GERAIS,
BRAZIL
Emerald

TREBNITZ,
CZECHOSLOVAKIA
Garnet

HABACHTHAL,
AUSTRIA
Emerald

ALA VALLEY,
PIEDMONT,
ITALY
Garnet

SISSERTSK,
URALS, USSR
Garnet

TAKOWAJA DISTRICT,
URALS, USSR
Alexandrite

SAYAN MTNS.,
LAKE BAIKAL
Nephrite

MALAYA
BYSTRAYA
USSR
Lapis

KUNLUN MTNS.,
CHINA
Nephrite

FENGTIEN, TAIWAN
Nephrite

CELEBES,
INDONESIA
Jadeite

OTAGO,
MT. COOK,
NEW ZEALAND
Nephrite

POONA
W. AUSTRALIA
Emerald

EYRE PENINSULA
AUSTRALIA
Nephrite

JEBEL SIKAIT,
EGYPT
Emerald

SAR-E-SANG,
BADAKSHAN,
AFGHANISTAN
Lapis

JAGDALEK,
AFGHANISTAN
Ruby

SWAT,
PAKISTAN
Emerald

HUNZA,
PAKISTAN
Ruby

KASHGAR,
PAKISTAN
Emerald

TAWMAW,
BURMA
Jadeite

MOGOK,
BURMA
Ruby
Spinel

JAIPUR,
INDIA
Garnet

MYSORE,
INDIA
Ruby

KALIGUMAN,
INDIA
Garnet

SARWAR,
INDIA
Garnet

MANGARI, KENYA
Ruby

TSAVO, KENYA
Garnet

LOSSOGONOI,
TANZANIA
Ruby

MOROGORO,
TANZANIA
Ruby

GILEVI HILLS,
UMBA TANZANIA
Ruby

AMPAINY, MADAGASCAR
Sapphire
Garnet

MUAGUIDE,
MOZAMBIQUE
Garnet

VICTORIA FIELD,
ZIMBABWE
Alexandrite

SANDAWANA,
ZIMBABWE
Emerald

NO. PARE MTNS.,
TANZANIA
Garnet

LONGIDO,
TANZANIA
Ruby

MANYARA,
TANZANIA
Emerald,
Alexandrite

KITWE,
ZAMBIA
Emerald

GRAVELOTTE,
TRANSVAAL,
SO. AFRICA
Emerald

BUFFELS-FONTEIN,
TRANSVAAL, SO. AFRICA
Garnet

○ LOW PRESSURE REGIONAL
   METAMORPHIC GEM DEPOSITS

△ HIGH PRESSURE REGIONAL
   METAMORPHIC GEM DEPOSITS

84

*M*any gemstones grow from fluids, in particular, water and molten rock. Others form in solid rock by a process known as metamorphism, which occurs when the temperature or pressure rises so high that the original minerals in the rock can no longer exist. With limited melting they gradually change to new minerals that can exist under the new conditions. Metamorphism commonly takes millions of years and may involve a small amount of water or limited melting. Most metamorphic gemstones result from either low-pressure (high-temperature) or high-pressure regional metamorphism, that is, metamorphism that occurs over a wide area.

Low-pressure (high-temperature) regional metamorphism typically occurs when two continents collide (Fig. 6-1). On the earth's surface a vast mountain range forms, such as the Himalayas where India once collided with the rest of Asia, and deep below the mountain range, where both temperature and pressure became extreme, metamorphism creates new minerals, including ruby, emerald, garnet, chrysoberyl, and nephrite jade. The most important low-pressure gem deposit is the Mogok ruby mine in northern Burma.

The high-pressure (low-temperature) type of regional metamorphism (referred to as blueschist metamorphism) commonly occurs where the ocean floor slides under the edge of a continent. As it moves down, the ocean crust is subjected to great pressure and undergoes metamorphism. Blocks of the ocean crust are broken off and pushed back up to the surface of the earth before they can become too hot. The minerals formed under these conditions are quite different from those formed during high-temperature regional metamorphism. Jadeite is the only important gemstone formed by this process.

The world's most important deposits of gem-quality jadeite are found in northern Burma, where veins of jadeite intermixed with albite feldspar occur on a plateau about 270 miles north of Mandalay. The best-known deposit is at Tawmaw. The jadeite was first recovered as stream-worn boulders from the riverbeds in the region, and later the source of the jadeite was found as veins in hard rock (Map 3).

6

Gemstones Formed by Low-Pressure Regional Metamorphism: The Ruby Deposits of Mogok, Burma

Low-pressure metamorphism can take place locally, as contact metamorphism, or over large areas, as regional metamorphism (Figure 6-1). When hot magma intrudes into the cool surrounding rock, the rock is heated and saturated by hydrothermal fluids and commonly undergoes change in the form of replacement of some of its component minerals or recrystallization of the entire rock mass. The type and degree of change are dependent upon the temperature and chemistry of the intruding magma and the type of rock subjected to the intrusion. Resistant, unreactive rocks, such as quartzites and sandstones, may go unchanged when invaded by the molten rock. Others, most dramatically carbonates such as limestones, may undergo tremendous change due to their chemical reactivity. If the carbonate rock is magnesium rich, such as dolomite, magnesium minerals such as diopside or serpentine form.

Likewise, the invading rock also contributes elements, the most common of which is silica.

Contact metamorphic gem deposits are commonly the result of granitic (silica-rich) magmas intruding into reactive carbonate rocks. However, some notable exceptions exist, the most important of which is when a silica-poor magma, such as a gabbro, invades aluminum-rich rocks such as shale and is desilicified. This desilicification in the presence of an abundance of aluminum allows the crystallization of aluminum oxides rather than aluminum silicates and hence the formation of corundum (ruby and sapphire).

Low-pressure (high-temperature) metamorphism can also take place on a much larger scale, not necessarily in proximity to igneous activity, and the mineral products of low-pressure regional metamorphism are very similar, if not identical in some instances, to those of contact metamorph-

Figure 6-1. Diagram showing the process of low-pressure regional metamorphism. Courtesy of the Natural History Museum of Los Angeles County.

ism. In fact, controversy surrounds the origin of some gem deposits, and the principal arguments center on the presence or absence of igneous activity nearby.

Lapis lazuli is a rare metamorphic rock with the mineral lazurite as an essential constitutent. Coarse-grained lazurite commonly occurs with diopside, marble, and pyrite, remote from any igneous rocks that could be related to its formation, and therefore low-pressure (high-grade) regional metamorphism is the process for its formation. Hogarth and Griffin (1978) suggest that such rocks represent metaevaporites that recrystallized during high-grade regional metamorphism. Afghanistan and Baffin Island are good examples of such deposits. Hogarth and Griffin (1980) point out, however, that lapis lazuli of much finer-grained texture can also be the result of contact-metamorphic activity around an intrusive igneous body, and they use the Italian Mountain area of Colorado as an example.

The Mogok ruby deposit in upper Burma is another controversial deposit that is reviewed in detail later in this chapter. Many gemology texts list Mogok as the result of contact metamorphism, yet the proper intrusive that could be responsible for the marbles that are interbedded with schists of unquestionably regional metamorphic origin is lacking.

Many other gem deposits are easily ascribed to regional metamorphism. Except for the Colombian deposits and perhaps those of Pakistan, most of the world's emerald deposits are the result of low-pressure regional metamorphic activity.

Low-pressure regional metamorphism commonly produces mica schists that may contain other minerals, including various species of garnet, ruby, and sapphire, as well as emerald and alexandrite chrysoberyl. In fact, the most common environment for emeralds on a worldwide basis is in schists. Occasionally, these schist-type emerald deposits also contain alexandrite chrysoberyl.

During regional metamorphism, granitic rocks including pegmatites are often mobilized, intrude the newly formed mica schists, and interact to form new minerals. As an example, Sinkankas (1981) states that emeralds and alexandrites in schist are the result of a chemical interaction induced when pegmatitic granitic rocks intrude silica-poor basic rocks such as a schist and the necessary chemical constituents for the emerald and alexandrite are transferred from the granite to the schist. Sinkankas terms this process *exometamorphism* because changes in the schist were the result of changes induced by outside constituents. The chromium necessary to induce the colors in the emerald and alexandrite was probably inherent in the schist.

The classic example of emerald in biotite schist is that on the east side of the Ural Mountains in the Soviet Union. Here, near the town of Sverdlovsk, a series of mines produce emeralds from mica schist. According to the Russian geologist Fersman, these deposits were the result of the "entrapment and compression of sediments between the acidic granite of the Western Zone massif and the basic and ultrabasic rocks of the Eastern Zone, both introducing chemical elements into the Central Zone which subsequently gave rise to the emerald-bearing biotite schists." The area also is famous for producing the world's finest alexandrites from these same biotite schists (Sinkankas, 1981).

Other important schist-type emerald deposits include the Miku deposit in Zambia (Hickman, 1972); Sandawana, Zimbabwe; Swat Valley, Pakistan (Gübelin, 1982); Habachtal, Austria; Poona, West Australia; Wadi Sikait, Egypt (MacAlister, 1900); Leysdorp, Transvaal, South Africa (LeGrange, 1929); Mewar, India (Roy, 1955); Lake Manyara, Tanzania (Gübelin, 1974; 1976a; 1976b); and Alexander County, North Carolina (Sinkankas, 1976).

One of the most interesting regional metamorphic gem areas, yet one of the least understood, is the East African gem belt of Kenya and Tanzania. The variety of gems found in this area is astounding. The Precambrian schists of East Africa have yielded ruby, emerald, alexandrite, chrome tourmaline, scapolite, and rhodolite garnet, as well as new gem species such as tanzanite and tsavolite garnet.

Nephrite jade also is the result of low-pressure regional metamorphism, probably on a localized scale. The nephrite deposits of Monterey County, California, and of Taiwan are generally thought to be the result of a metasomatic product of serpentinate derived from an ultramafic rock such as peridotite.

Similar nephrite occurrences are found in the Kunlun Mountains of Xinjang Autonomous Region, China; New Zealand; the Soviet Union; Taiwan; and Alaska, Canada, California, and Wyoming in North America.

Several major corundum deposits, including the ruby deposits in India, East Africa, and the Hunza Valley, Pakistan, have been formed by low-pressure regional metamorphism. Discussion of the origin of these deposits pits regional metamorphic origin versus localized contact metamorphism (Gübelin, 1982; Okrusch et al., 1976). One of the best examples of this controversy, as well as one of the most important gem-producing areas in the world, is the ruby and spinel mines of the Mogok Stone Tract in Burma.

When a granitic intrusion comes in contact with limestone containing aluminum-rich impurities, it is recrystallized into coarse calcite crystals to form a crystalline limestone or marble. Any impurities such as aluminum also crystallize into new aluminum minerals such as corundum (Al_2O_3). If the limestone is dolomitic, that is, additionally contains abundant magnesium, spinel ($MgAl_2O_4$) may form in place of corundum. This has been the classic explanation at Mogok, Burma, where some

of the world's finest rubies and spinels have been recovered. Limestone subjected to low-pressure regional metamorphism would give rise to very similar rocks. More detailed examinations of the deposit are obviously required.

THE RUBY DEPOSITS OF MOGOK, BURMA

Any list of the classic, historically most important gem deposits of the world must include the Mogok Stone Tract in Upper Burma. Mogok has been associated with the world's finest rubies for more than four centuries, but not until the British assumed control of Burma in 1886 was Mogok's potential for producing beautiful, deep crimson (pigeon blood) rubies truly realized (Fig. 6-2). Although Mogok is known particularly for these fine rubies, quantities of fine sapphires, spinels, and peridots are also found there. Sapphires are most abundant in the nearby Kathe, Kyatpyin, and Gwebin deposits; peridot is limited to the area of Bernardmyo some 10 km north-northwest of the village of Mogok. Also found in gem quality in the Mogok area are apatite, scapolite, moonstone, zircon, garnet, iolite, and amethyst.

Historical records indicate that the Mogok Stone Tract has been worked since at least 1597 A.D., when the king of Burma secured the mines from the local Shan ruler. After the British annexation of Upper Burma in 1886, the mines were leased to a British firm, which organized Burma Ruby Mines, Ltd. Although the British firm used modern methods to work the mines, profitability was sporadic at best. Burma Ruby Mines worked the area until the early 1930s when Mogok reverted back to native mining and the methods used for hundreds of years before the arrival of the British.

Today, little information comes out of Burma regarding the Mogok Stone Tract. Since 1962, when the Socialist regime took power and subsequently nationalized all industry including gem mining, few foreigners have been allowed to visit Mogok. During this period, supplies of rubies from Burma have diminished drastically. Although some stones are sold at annual auctions in Rangoon, the few high-quality gems that emerge are smuggled out through Thailand.

Because of this isolation, research for this chapter consists of a thorough review of the literature as well as interviews with people who had visited Mogok prior to 1962. The photos, which

Figure 6-2. *This extraordinary 10.02-carat ruby ring and the accompanying 14.54-carat (total weight) ruby earrings are superb examples of Burmese rubies. From the Ballreich and Kantor collection. Photo by Harold and Erica Van Pelt.*

come from some of these same people, are particularly rare. The literature is rich in information on Mogok, usually based on a visit to the area by some Western gem dealer. The first such report was that of Pierre d'Amato (1833), who described the local mining methods in the Mogok area. Since then many articles have been written, principally on the mining activities (Wynne, 1897; Morgan, 1904; Gordon, 1888; Scott, 1936). Since the 1965 article by Gübelin, who also produced a superb 2-hour documentary film on the area, however, noth-

ing of importance has been contributed to the modern literature.

Location and Access

The Mogok Stone Tract is located in the Kathe district of Upper Burma between latitudes 22°50′45″ N to 23°5′15″ N and longitudes 96°19′ E to 96°35′ E, or approximately 700 km north of the Burmese capital of Rangoon. Mogok (Figure 6-3) is about 150 km NE of Mandalay, and is located at an elevation of about 1,200 m (4,000 feet). It is the major population cen-

Figure 6-3. *A view of the town of Mogok comes from across the artificial lake that resulted from the flooding of the extensive works of the Burma Ruby Mines, Ltd. Photo by Edward Gübelin.*

ter in the area, with 6,000 inhabitants reported in 1960 (Meen 1962). The tract is about 1,040 square kilometers in extent and includes the townships of Kyatpyin, Kathe, and Mogok.

The general area of the tract is very mountainous, forming the western borders of the Shan Plateau. Most of the mining takes place in the alluvia of floors and flanks of the Mogok, Kyatpyin, Kathe, and Luda valleys. Mogok Valley is the most important, consisting of a narrow alluvial plain, 5 km long running NE-SW, and about 1 km wide.

All reports of travel to Mogok, when it was permitted, indicate that access to the mining area was very difficult. According to Ehrman (1957), there were two principal travel alternatives. The first started with three days by train from Rangoon to Mandalay, followed by two days of boat travel up the Irrawaddy River to Thabeikkyin, where one could hire a car for the final 95 tortuous kilometers. The second, and far easier, means was a four-to-six-hour flight from Rangoon to Momeik via Union of Burma Airways, then about 40 km by jeep from Momeik to Mogok.

Because the current Burmese government limits foreign visitors to a 24-hour visa, any travel into the interior is virtually impossible. In addition, the Mogok area is under military control and visits by foreigners are forbidden (Nordland, 1982).

History and Production

According to Webster (1975), the earliest historical record of Mogok shows that the mines were taken over by the king of Burma in 1597 from the local ruling Shan in exchange for the town of Mong Mit (Momeik) some 40 km away. The descendants of the king worked the mines intermittently. In 1780, King Bodawgyi operated the mines with slave labor. Shortly thereafter, the king placed control of the Mogok mines in the hands of governors (Sos) who allowed mining on payment of a tax. Valuable stones remained the property of the king, however, with no compensation to the miner. This period was one of great oppression, and many miners left the region. The area never really recovered, and by the 1870s conditions were so intolerable that King Thebaw began negotiating with outside companies to work the deposits. He eventually leased mining rights to the Burmah [sic] and Bombay Trading Company but arbitrarily canceled their lease on the ruby mines in 1882 (*Mineral Resources*, 1886). This action, along with certain provocations to the British-controlled lumber industry, led the British to invade Upper Burma in 1886 with an army of 30,000 men (*Mineral Resources*, 1886). The British

annexed Upper Burma to the colony of India that same year. In October 1887, the Upper Burma Ruby Regulations were promulgated, creating the so-called stone tracts. In November of that year, the Mogok Stone Tract was established (Chhibber, 1934a and 1934b). In 1889, the British government, through the secretary of state for India, awarded control of the Mogok mines to Edwin Streeter, the eminent Bond Street (London) jeweler, who organized Burma Ruby Mines, Ltd. The initial 1889 lease of the mining rights to the 10- by 20-mile (15- by 30-km) tract was for a 7-year period at an annual rent of 26,666 pounds plus 16.66% of the net profits (Adams, 1926).

When Burma Ruby Mines, Ltd., moved into Mogok, it faced severe difficulties, not the least of which was that the richest deposits were under the village of Mogok itself. Before mining could begin, the entire village had to be moved to its present location. In the years that followed, the company also had to build roads, bridges, buildings, five washing mills, and a 400-kw hydroelectric plant. In addition, the company was plagued by the age-old problem of miners "highgrading" and smuggling a large percentage of the gem production (Brown, 1933). The Indian government protected the local miners, stating that Burma Ruby Mines could not disturb established native miners in their work, nor remove them except by purchase of their claims. Otherwise, the British company held a monopoly on the mining rights of the Mogok Stone Tract (Adams, 1926; Calhoun, 1929).

In 1896, the original 7-year lease was renewed and extended for 14 years wiith a fixed rental fee of 13,333 pounds plus 30% of the net profit per year. The mining of rubies in Mogok was at an all-time high. Five large washing mills processed thousands of tons of earth each day. The area eventually became so prosperous that more mills were erected 12 km from Mogok, near Kyatpyin. All mining was open pit, using large hydraulic monitors, or "cannons," under high pressure to wash gem gravels through a series of sluice boxes (Webster, 1975).

The area prospered under the control of the Burma Ruby Mines until 1908, when large numbers of synthetic rubies entered the world gem market and caused immediate panic among ruby buyers worldwide. Sales of rubies declined dramatically. Although the Mogok operations continued all through World War I, in 1925 Burma Ruby Mines went into voluntary liquidation (Brown, 1933). The company had 6 years remaining on its lease, however, and struggled on until 1931, when it surrendered the lease to the government (Halford-Watkins, 1932).

Keely (1982), one of the managers of the mine, gave some additional insight into the decline of modern mining in the Mogok area. He pointed out that exceptionally heavy rainfall in 1929 caused severe flooding, which destroyed all of the electric pumps as well as the drainage tunnels used to keep the mines from being inundated. The large lake formed by the flooding still remains today. Several attempts were made to repair the flood damage but with no success. Furthermore, as the modern techniques were no longer considered economic, the native miners and their centuries-old mining methods took over Mogok once again. All lease restrictions with respect to applications for licenses were removed, and the government simply collected 10 rupees per month from each miner to cover the cost of a license that the miner "was to wear on the seat of his pants" (Halford-Watkins, 1932). Local mining continued except from May 1942 to March 1945, when the Japanese occupied Burma and the Mogok tract became part of the battleground of the United States Fourteenth Army and the Japanese. After World War II, local mining prospered until the nationalization of the mines by the Socialist regime in 1963.

When the Burmese government nationalized all industries in 1963, it forbade all private businesses, including gem mining and selling. Today, the diminished gem mining is monitored by the army, and gems can be sold legally only at the annual auction held in Rangoon by the MYANMA Export Import Corporation, whose subdivision is the Burma Gems, Jade, and Pearl Emporium. These auctions have not been highly successful because of the generally poor quality of the stones offered. The total sales figures from the annual gem emporium, as published by the *Minerals Yearbook*, give some idea of modern production. In 1969, the Fifth Annual Gem Emporium yielded $2,400,000. This figure rose dramatically in 1973 to $5,800,000, the last year for which statistics are available, but this sum represents mostly income from sales of jade and pearls, with very few rubies having been offered.

Early production records are difficult to find and generally incomplete. According to Iyer (1953), in a table of production statistics for the Burma Ruby Mines, Ltd., 1,300,000 carats of ruby were recovered from 1924 to 1939. As usual with gem-production statistics, how much additional material was recovered by highgraders and operators of private claims is not known.

According to Nordland (1982), the Mogok area is off-limits to foreigners and closed even to Burmese without special permission. A division of Bur-

mese troops now oversees the government-owned mines.

Geology

Several detailed accounts of the geology of the Mogok Stone Tract have been published. The earliest is the large, comprehensive work of Brown and Judd (1896), who conducted their study on behalf of the Burma Ruby Mines, Ltd., and the secretary of state for India. La Touche, perhaps best known for his work on the Kashmir sapphire mines, included the Mogok area in his *Geology of the Northern Shan States* (La Touche, 1913). Other early geologic studies include Bleeck (1908), Fermor (1930, 1931, 1932, 1934, and 1935), and Heron (1936 and 1937). Chhibber (1934a) includes a description of the gem gravels in his work on the geology of Burma.

Systematic mapping of the Mogok Stone Tract on a scale of 4 inches = 1 mile was started in 1929 and published by Brown (1933). Much more extensive mapping was continued by Iyer (1953). This work, by far the most complete on the Mogok area, resulted in a superb map of the deposit (Fig. 6-4).

As is the case with all tropical areas, the geologic mapping of Mogok was difficult. The geologist must not only contend with dense vegetation and numerous wild animals but also study rocks that are covered with a thick mantle of soil and products of deep chemical weathering. In the Mogok area, annual rainfall is more than 360 cm (140 inches).

The geology of the Mogok area is very complex, consisting primarily of high-grade metamorphic schists and gneisses; granite intrusives, including gem-bearing pegmatites; peridot-bearing ultramafic rocks; and, most importantly, ruby- and spinel-bearing metamorphic marble.

The rubies of Mogok are weathered from the marble of the area, which is in contact or interbedded with a complex series of highly folded gneissic rocks. Iyer (1953) identified 13 mappable rock units in the Mogok area. These, however, can be, and often are, grouped into: (1) intrusive granitic rocks; (2) the Mogok gneiss, which consists of metamorphic schists and gneisses; (3) the Pleistocene and recent (Quaternary) alluvium; (4) ultramafic intrusives; and (5) marbles.

The Mogok gneiss is the prevalent rock unit in the region. It consists of many types of metamorphic rocks, including scapolite- and garnet-rich biotite gneisses, calc-granulites, quartzites, garnet- and sillimanite-rich gneisses, and hornblende schists and gneisses. The Mogok gneiss makes up

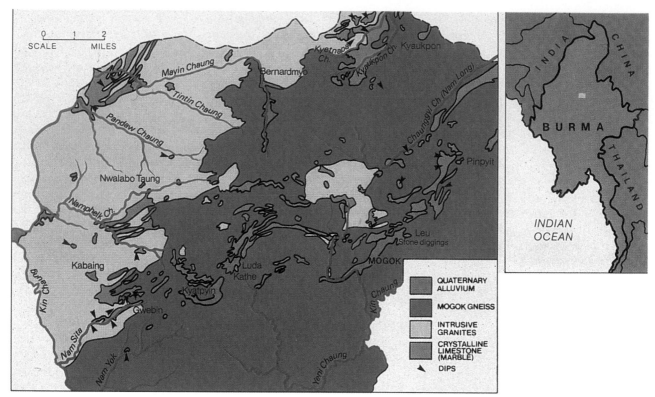

Figure 6-4. Detailed geologic map of the Mogok Stone Tract of Burma, adapted from the original drawn by Clegg and Iyer (Iyer, 1953).

the eastern two-thirds of the area mapped by Clegg and Iyer (Iyer, 1953). The marbles, which are the host rocks of the rubies and spinels, are intimately interbedded with the Mogok gneiss. Rounded fragments of the Mogok gneiss are a major constituent of the gem gravels. Because of the heavy rainfall and tropical climate of the region, the Mogok gneiss weathers very quickly to a reddish lateritic soil, leaving only rounded boulder remnants.

The granitic intrusives in the Mogok area form most of the western third of the stone tract. On Clegg and Iyer's detailed geologic map (Iyer, 1953), they consist of the Kabaing granite, an augite and hornblende granite, a syenite, and a tourmaline granite. Pegmatites containing topaz, tourmaline, and aquamarine are also included in this map unit. Many small exposures of granitic rock have been included in the unclassified crystallines of the Mogok gneiss.

Of the granitic intrusives mapped by Clegg and Iyer, the Kabaing granite is by far the most important and one of the largest rock units in the area. It is found in workings throughout the Mogok area, and much of the gravel encountered in the alluvium is undoubtedly derived from this granite.

The Kabaing granite contains numerous quartz- and topaz-bearing pegmatites, with cassit-

erite noted in abundance in certain of these bodies. Iyer (1953) states that the two topaz crystals weighing about 5 kg each were kept in the office of the Burma Geologic Survey. Such gem minerals, along with large quartz crystals, were generally sold to Chinese traders for carving.

In the Mogok area, basic intrusives are very rare and limited to gabbros and hornblende-pyroxene rocks, as well as to peridotites found as minor intrusive dikes and sills principally in the Bernardmyo area about 10 km north of Mogok. These rocks are of minor importance, except when they are the source of the spectacular Burmese gem peridot, which rivals that from Zabargad (St. John's Island), Egypt. The peridotite in the Bernardmyo area is a light-colored, granular rock composed almost entirely of olivine with minor pyroxene and magnetite (Iyer, 1953). In the peridot diggings, the rock is generally seen only as a series of loose, weathered boulders with serpentinization along fracture surfaces. Also included as a minor map unit along with the ultramafic intrusives is a small outcrop of nepheline syenite about 12 km west of Mogok.

The marble is generally very coarsely crystallized and pure white in color, although locally it may be tinged with yellow or pink. In addition to ruby and spinel, the marble contains diopside, phlogopite, forsterite, chondrodite, scapolite, sphene, garnet, and graphite. The marble has been intruded by granitic rocks, and the effects of contact metamorphism are evidenced by the presence of feldspar and diopside in very coarse-grained portions that are in contact with the granitic rocks.

La Touche (1913) included the marbles as part of the Mogok gneiss; Iyer (1953) chose to place the marbles in the "Mogok Series," restricting the Mogok gneiss to gneisses and unclassified crystalline rocks. These unclassified crystalline rocks consist of gneisses, granites, and quartz veins that, because of the thick soil horizon and dense jungle, could not be mapped as separate units.

In the valleys and on the sides of the hills, the gem-bearing gravel layer rests on a soft, decomposed rock of characteristic appearance. This gem-bearing bed consists for the most part of brown or yellow, more or less firm, clayey, and at times sandy material, known locally as *byon* (Cecil, 1928). This layer, the residuum left by solution of the marble during weathering, contains ruby, sapphire, and other varieties of colored corundum, as well as spinel, quartz, tourmaline, feldspar grains, nodules of weathered pyrite, and other minerals of lesser importance. Rarely, a pure gem sand occurs; it consists almost entirely of minute, sparkling grains of ruby. The byon lies, as a rule, from 5 to 6 m below the surface of the valley floor and is from 1 to 2 m in thickness, pinching off to nil. On the sides of the valley, the beds of byon are as thick as 15 to 22 m. These are, of course, purely residual weathering deposits (Chhibber, 1934a).

Mining Methods

After the departure of the British and their modern mining techniques, Burmese mining was very active, with operations varying in size from single operators to mines employing two to three dozen workers.

The indigenous mining methods used at Mogok have been described in great detail (Simpson, 1922; Adams, 1926; Halford-Watkins, 1932; Iyer, 1953; Spaulding, 1956; Ehrmann, 1957; Meen, 1962; Gübelin, 1965). The three most common mining methods described by these authors include the *twinlon* (twin), the *hmyadwin* (hmyaw), and the *loodwin* (loo).

A twinlon, usually constructed in the dry season, consists of a small circular pit that in general is less than 1 m in diameter (Fig. 6-5). These pits are commonly 6 to 12 m deep, although some as deep as 30 m have been reported (Halford-Watkins, 1932). The pits are dug vertically until the gem gravel or byon is reached. The miners then dig laterally for about a 10- to 12-m radius to remove the gem-bearing gravel. The pits are illuminated by means of a mirror from above. Commonly, three men work in a single twinlon: Two men dig while the third uses a long bamboo crane with a basket attached to haul up the earth. This method is not unlike that employed at the Ban Kha Cha sapphire deposit near Chanthaburi, Thailand (Chapter 5; Keller, 1983). Occasionally, when water is a problem, a *lebin*, that is, a 1- to 2-meter square pit, is constructed and reinforced with timber. Water is removed via a bamboo pump. The recovered gem

Figure 6-5. A twinlon, or circular pit, from which gem-bearing gravel is removed via the basket attached to the long bamboo crane shown here. Photo by Edward Gübelin.

gravels are then carefully washed and sorted on the surface.

The second most common method of recovering gems at Mogok is by means of a quarrylike hmyadwin, or hmyaw. These open-pit mines are usually worked during the rainy season, because they employ hydraulic mining and require a great deal of water. A hmyadwin is dug into a hillside to a depth of 6 to 15 m. Hmyadwins are usually used continuously for 50 to 60 years because of their very complicated construction. They vary greatly in size, but the most complex uses a series of channels to bring in water from great distances to wash the soil and gem gravels removed from open-pit mining on the hillside. The gravels and much lighter wastes are washed into flat, circular stone pits, where the "heavies" are trapped in a series of sluices. The lighter wastes are washed into the valley below. During operation, large pebbles are picked out and discarded, and the sluices are periodically inspected for gems (Fig. 6-6).

Deep chemical weathering in the limestone areas of Mogok produces typical karst topography, including numerous underground caverns that may go for hundreds of meters and contain huge chambers lined with spectacular stalactites and stalagmites. Such caverns, called *loodwins* or *loos*, may also contain some of the richest gem gravels in the Mogok Stone Tract. Unfortunately, mining in these caverns is the most dangerous of the three methods. A miner must find a way through very narrow channels in the limestone while digging in every crevice for gem gravel, which is put in a basket dragged on one foot. When the basket is full, it is brought to the surface and the gravel is washed. Because of natural concentration in the loos, such gravel may contain up to 25% ruby (Chhibber, 1934b). However, miners not uncommonly get stuck in the rocks or lost underground. Because of this danger, as well as the depletion of accessible loos, this method has been used only rarely in recent years.

As is the practice in most of the gem-producing areas of the world, once the miner finishes processing the gravel and abandons it, it is freely available to the small independent miner (Fig. 6-7), who may reprocess it in the hope of finding overlooked gem material. In the case of Mogok, however, only women are allowed to search for gems in such refuse. These women, called *kanase*, usually recover only enough from the debris to live on, but they have been known to recover large gems.

Figure 6-6. A recovery and washing plant for gem gravels near Mogok. Photo by Edward Gübelin.

Famous Rubies from Mogok

Unlike diamond, emerald, and sapphire, fine, well-publicized, faceted Burmese rubies are almost unknown. In fact, few if any named rubies are in the museums or royal treasuries of the world today. Gemological literature of the twentieth century does note a handful of stones exceeding 5 carats, but with the exception of two—the 43-carat Peace ruby and the approximately 40-carat Chhatrapati Manick (Clarke, 1933)—no others were significant enough to bear names, and even the whereabouts of the two named stones is unknown today.

In 1875, owing to the impoverished condition of the ruling house of Burma, two spectacular rubies were placed on the market. After cutting, these stones weighed 32.35 and 38.55 carats. Seldom have two such remarkable and perfect rubies appeared on the European market simultaneously. These two stones brought 10,000 pounds and 20,000 pounds, respectively. At the time, many regarded this incident as only an indicator of the quality and size of the gems that the ruling houses of these eastern empires must possess. Yet, when the British conquered and annexed Burma, they found little or no evidence of vast stores of corundum gems, although the possibility exists that all the royal gems were stolen during the conquest of the country, by both the Burmese and the British (Brown, 1934).

Figure 6-7. As is the case in most gem-mining operations, the waste from the major mining operations is freely available to independent miners for sorting. In Burma, however, this sorting is limited to females, known locally as kanase. *Photo by Edward Gübelin.*

Figure 6-8. One of the finest Burmese ruby crystals ever placed on public display is this 196.1-carat etched crystal, which is now part of the Hixon collection of the Natural History Museum of Los Angeles County. Photo by Harold and Erica Van Pelt.

Figure 6-9. This 15.97-carat cushion-cut ruby from the Mogok Stone Tract is considered to be one of the finest Burmese rubies known today. Photo © 1988 Tino Hammid.

Years later, in 1899, a 77-carat rough ruby was discovered by Burma Ruby Mines, Ltd. The most famous Burma ruby was found on Armistice Day, November 11, 1918. Two English mine supervisors spotted the stone on the washing pan and called for the mine's general manager, who subsequently named it the Peace ruby (Keely, 1982). The 43-carat crystal reportedly was purchased by a wealthy Mogok stone merchant who cut it into a 22-carat flawless stone. Unfortunately, its color tone was slightly dark, and the cut gem sold for less than the dealer had paid for the crystal. Since the discovery of the Chhatrapati Manick and the Peace Ruby, several stones of nearly 30 carats have been found, although none has received a special name that has been carried into the literature.

Today, fine Burmese rubies are almost nonexistent in museum collections. The British Museum of Natural History at South Kensington displays the 167-carat Edwards ruby crystal, which was given to the museum by John Ruskin in 1887 (Spencer, 1933). The crystal is not of faceting quality, but must be considered one of the more important Burmese rubies surviving today. The Natural His-

tory Museum of Los Angeles County displays the 196.1-carat Hixon ruby (Fig. 6-8). This highly etched crystal is of superb color and possesses unusually complete crystal form. Allan Caplan, a New York gem dealer, had a magnificent 15.97-carat faceted Burma ruby that many believe is one of the finest rubies of its kind. It is exceptionally free of flaws and has the classic pigeon blood color (Fig. 6-9). It was displayed at the American Museum of Natural History in New York and recently sold at auction for the highest price per carat of any colored gemstone in history.

REFERENCES

Adams, F. D. 1926. A visit to the gem districts of Ceylon and Burma. *Bulletin of the Canadian Institute of Mining and Metallurgy* 166:213–246.

Anderson, B. W. 1980. *Gem Testing.* Butterworths, London.

Bank, H., and E. Gübelin. 1976. Das Smaragd-Alexandritvorkommen von Lake Manyara/Tanzania. *Zeitschrift der Deutschen Gemmologischen Gesellschaft* 25(3):130–147.

Bleeck, A. W. G. 1908. Rubies in the Kachin Hills, Upper Burma. *Records of the Geological Survey of India* 36:164–170.

Brown, C. B., and J. W. Judd. 1896. The rubies of Burma and associated minerals; their mode of occurrence, origin and metamorphoses: A contribution to the history of corundum. *Philosophical Transactions of the Royal Society of London.* Series A 187:151–228.

Brown, J. C. 1933. Ruby mining in Upper Burma. *Mineralogical Magazine and Journal of the Mineralogical Society* 48(6):329–340.

Brown, J. C. 1934. Mining rubies in Burma. *Gemmologist* 3(31):199–203.

Calhoun, A. B. 1929. Burma: An important source of precious and semiprecious gems. *Engineering and Mining Journal* 127(18):708–712.

Cecil, G. 1928. Ruby mining in Burma. *Engineering and Mining Journal* 127(8):294.

Chhibber, H. L. 1934a. *The Geology of Burma.* Macmillan and Co., London.

Chhibber, H. L. 1934b. *The Mineral Resources of Burma.* Macmillan and Co., London.

Clarke, V. 1933. The story of an Indian ruby. *Gemmologist* 2:148–153.

d'Amato, P. G. 1833. A short description of the mines of precious stones in the district of Kyatpyin, in the Kingdom of Ava. *Journal of the Asiatic Society of Bengal* 2:75–76.

Ehrman, M. 1957. Gem mining in Burma. *Gems & Gemology* 9(1):3–30

Eppler, W. F. 1976. Negative crystals in ruby from Burma. *Journal of Gemmology* 15(1):1–5.

Fermor, L. L. 1930. Mineral production of India during 1929. *Records of the Geological Survey of India* 63(3):281–357.

Fermor, L. L. 1931. Mogok stone tract, Katha district. *Records of the Geological Survey of India* 65(1):80–86, 90–95.

Fermor, L. L. 1932. The Mogok stone tract, Katha district. *Records of the Geological Survey of India* 66(1):92–96.

Fermor, L. L. 1934. Mogok stone tract. *Records of the Geological Survey of India* 68(1):50–58.

Fermor, L. L. 1935. Mogok stone tract. *Records of the Geological Survey of India* 69(1):50–54.

Gordon, R. 1888. On the ruby mines near Mogok, Burma. *Proceedings of the Royal Geographic Society* 10:261–275.

Gübelin, E. 1965. The ruby mines in Mogok, Burma. *Journal of Gemmology* 9(12):411–427.

Gübelin, E. 1974. The emerald deposit at Lake Manyara, Tanzania. *The Lapidary Journal,* No. 5.

Gübelin, E. 1982. Gemstones of Pakistan: Emerald, ruby, and spinel. *Gems & Gemology* 18(3):123–139.

Halford-Watkins, J. F. 1932. Methods of ruby mining in Burma. *Gemmologist* 1(11):335–342; 12:367–373.

Heron, A. M. 1936. Mogok stone tract. *Records of the Geological Survey of India* 71(1):58–63.

Heron, A. M. 1937. Age of Mogok series. *Records of the Geological Survey of India* 72(1):62.

Hickman, A. C. J. 1972. *The Miku Emerald Deposit.* Economic report 27 of the Republic of Zambia, Ministry of Mines and Mining Department. Geological Survey.

Hogarth, D. D., and W. L. Griffin. 1978. Lapis lazuli from Baffin Island: A Precambrian meta-evaporite. *Lithos* 11:37–60.

Hogarth, D. D., and W. L. Griffin. 1980. Contact—Metamorphic lapis lazuli: The Italian Mountain deposits, Colorado. *Canadian Mineralogist* 18:59–70.

Iyer, L. A. N. 1953. The geology and gem-stones of the Mogok stone tract, Burma. *Memoirs of the Geological Survey of India* 82:100.

Keely, H. H. 1982. The ruby mines of Burma. *Gems* 14(3):6–11; 4:10–14.

Keller, P. C. 1982. The Chanthaburi-Trat gem field, Thailand. *Gems & Gemology* 18(4):186–196.

Keller, P. C. 1983. The rubies of Burma: A review of the Mogok stone tract. *Gems & Gemology* 19(4):209–219.

La Touche, T. H. D. 1913. Geology of the Northern Shan States. *Memoirs of the Geological Survey of India* 39(2):379.

LeGrange, J. M. 1929. The Barbara beryls: A study of an occurrence of emeralds in the north-eastern Transvaal . . . in the Murchison Range. *Transactions of the Geological Society of South Africa* 32:1–25.

MacAlister, D. 1900. The emerald mines of northern Etbai. *Geographical Journal* (London) 16:537–549.

Meen, M. A. 1962. Gem hunting in Burma. *Lapidary Journal* 16(7):636–653.

Mineral Resources. 1886. U.S. Geological Survey, Washington, D.C.

Morgan, A. H. 1904. The ruby mines of Burma. *Mining Journal* 16:4.

Nordland, R. 1982. On the treacherous trail to the rare ruby red. *Asia* 5(3):34–55.

Okrusch, M., T. E. Bunch, and H. Bank. 1976. Paragenesis and petrogenesis of a corundum-bearing marble at Hunza (Kashmire). *Mineralium Deposita* 11:278–297.

Roy, B. C. 1955. Emerald deposits in Mewar and Ajmer Merwara. *Records of the Geological Survey of India* 86:377–401.

Scott, W. H. 1936. The ruby mines of Burma. *Gems & Gemology* 2(1):3–6.

Simpson, R. R. 1922. Notes on a visit to the Burma ruby mines. *Transactions of the Mining and Geological Institute* 17(1):42–58.

Sinkankas, J. 1976. *Gemstones of North America.* 2 vols. Van Nostrand Reinhold Company, New York.

Sinkankas, J. 1981. *Emerald and Other Beryls.* Chilton Book Co., Radnor, Pa. 665 pages.

Spaulding, D. L. 1956. The ruby mines of Mogok, Burma. *Gems & Gemology* 8(11):335–342.

Spencer, L. J. 1933. Nation acquires large ruby. *Gemmologist* 2(18):176–178.

Webster, R. 1975. *Gems: Their Sources, Descriptions, and Identification.* 3d ed. Butterworths, London.

Wynne, T. T. 1897. The ruby mines of Burma. *Transactions of the Institute of Mining and Metallurgy* 5:161–175.

7

Gemstones Formed by High-Pressure Regional Metamorphism: The Jadeite Deposits of Tawmaw, Burma

Two tough, compact, fine-grained materials, jadeite and nephrite, are forms of the gem material jade. Composition by itself, however, does not define jade. It must also have a texture that gives it extreme toughness. Despite their similar properties, jadeite and nephrite are distinct materials with different compositions and textures.

Jadeite (sodium aluminum silicate) is a mineral belonging to the group called *pyroxenes.* Nephrite belongs to the amphibole mineral group and ranges between the amphibolite tremolite (calcium magnesium silicate) and actinolite (calcium iron silicate). Traditionally, the term "jade" is often incorrectly applied to any massive green stone suitable for carving. Nephrite is the product of low-pressure regional or contact metamorphism. It consists of microscopic interlocking fibrous crystals (Fig. 7-1).

Jadeite jade is a very tough mineral composed of many tiny, interlocking, granular crystals.

Formed by high-pressure regional metamorphism (Fig. 7-2), it can display a variety of colors due to trace amounts of elements such as chromium and iron or inclusions of other minerals such as hematite.

High-pressure regional metamorphism occurs where rocks are subjected to very deep burial but relatively low temperature. The minerals formed under these conditions are quite different from those formed during low-pressure regional metamorphism. Jadeite jade is the only important gemstone of this group.

When the ocean floor slides under the edge of a continent, it is subjected to very high pressure, but the temperatures remain low because the ocean floor starts out quite cool. During the process, which occurs over millions of years, the basalts of the ocean floor are broken off and pushed back to the earth's surface forming high-pressure recrystallization (Fig. 7-3). The resulting rocks are

101

Figure 7-1. A thin section of nephrite shows interwoven fibrous crystals magnified 100 times. Photo courtesy of the Smithsonian Institution (NMNH #R6775).

Figure 7-2. A thin section of jadeite shows many interlocking granular crystals. Magnified 100 times. Photo courtesy of the Smithsonian Institution (NMNH #94303).

defined as *glaucophane schists* or *blueschists.* Characterized by the stability of the jadeite-quartz assemblage and glaucophane, these rocks are geologically limited to compressional zones associated with lithospheric plate boundaries where subduction and obduction are active. Experimental work on blueschist minerals including jadeite and glaucophane suggest necessary pressures as high as 5 to 7 kilobars and temperatures of about 150° to 300°C. The typical reaction is jadeite plus quartz equals albite. Jadeite can form at somewhat lower pressures in the absence of quartz, but as Turner (1981) points out, pure jadeite as a tectonic block is quite rare and best documented from Clear Creek in San Benito County, California. At Clear Creek jadeite forms nongem blocks up to 2 meters across and is completely enclosed in serpentinite. It is always associated with albite but never quartz. Turner (1981) suggests that the silica may be lost to enclosing serpentinite that acts as a silica sink. This sort of desilication reaction could produce pure jadeite from albite. This is the condition observed in the Tawmaw, Burma, area.

Jadeite occurrences are quite rare on a worldwide basis, particularly jadeite of gem quality. Scattered reports of jadeite in Yunnan Province, China, and in Tibet probably represent trading centers for material coming out of Burma. Jadeite has been observed near the village of Kotaki in Niigata Pre-

fecture, in Japan, but it is of poor quality (Chihara, 1971; Iwao, 1953). Similar jadeite was recently reported from the Ural and Borus Mountains in the Soviet Union (Desautels, 1986). Jadeite of mineralogical interest has been discovered in several counties in California. In the mid-1930s boulders and nodules of jadeite in serpentinite noted earlier were found near Clear Creek in southwestern San Benito County, California, with pumpellyite and lawsonite. Similar occurrences were since noted in Mendocino, Trinity, San Luis Obispo, and Sonoma counties, all in glaucophane schists. Mineralogically interesting specimens of jadeite occur along the Russian River near Cloverdale in Sonoma County.

More important occurrences of jadeite have been found in the Celebes (DeRoever, 1955) and in Guatemala (Foshag, 1957; Foshag et al., 1955). Pre-Columbian jadeite artifacts have been found throughout Central America and Mexico for many years, but the source was unknown. In the 1950s, however, an outcrop of in situ jadeite was found above the village of Manzanal in Guatemala. Recent work has confirmed this observation and found other outcrops on the north side of the Motagua River, particularly along the valley of the Palmilla River, a tributary of the Motagua (McBirney et al., 1967). Recently, outcrops have also been noted west of the Palmilla River stretching all the way to

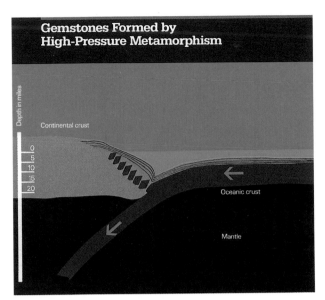

Gemstones Formed by High-Pressure Metamorphism

Figure 7-3. Diagram showing process of high-pressure regional metamorphism. Courtesy of the Natural History Museum of Los Angeles County.

the Huijo River (Desautels, 1986). The only major deposit of gem-quality jadeite occurs in the Tawmaw area of northern Burma, however.

THE JADEITE DEPOSITS OF TAWMAW, BURMA

Location and Access

The Hpakan-Tawmaw jade tract is the most important jadeite-producing area in the world (Gübelin, 1965, 1976). It is situated in the Kachin Hills of the far western Myitkyina district of northern Burma, about 70 miles northwest of the town of Mogaung, an important jade-cutting and trading center, and approximately 120 miles north of Mandalay. The approximately 800-square-mile mining area is bounded on the east by the Uru River and the west by the Chindwin River. The north and south are bounded by the twenty-fifth and twenty-sixth parallels of latitude, respectively (Soe-Win, 1968). The center of the mining area is the village of Tawmaw, situated on a 1,500- to 2,000-foot-high plateau that extends for about 10 miles in a north-south direction but is less than one mile wide. Of the many individual mines in the area, the most important are the Khaisumaw, Merchant, Chater, and the Yihkumaw group of mines. All of these mines are recovering jadeite from primary deposits. Alluvial mining also takes place in the neighborhood of Tawmaw Hill and in the portion of the Uru River flanking Tawmaw Hill.

Access to the area has always been limited to unimproved roads that are usable only during the dry season, which usually extends from March through May. Mule and horses are still the most efficient means of transportation, although Jeeps have been used to reach some areas. Since the Socialist government took power in 1963, few if any Westerners have visited the Tawmaw area. Meen (1962) gives a detailed account of what a visit to the region entailed during what was possibly the last visit by a Westerner to the area.

History

Nephrite jade has been sought after and revered by the Chinese for thousands of years. Not until the late eighteenth century did the rarer jadeite jade begin to make an impact on the Chinese jade market, even though jadeite was reportedly recovered from the Tawmaw area as "serpentinite" since the thirteenth century. Details of its discovery are uncertain. According to Scalisi and Cook (1983), a Yunnanese trader inadvertently used a jadeite boulder to balance his mule's load while crossing the Burma-China frontier. Reportedly, "jadeite" trickled into China from Burma for the next 500 years. If this is true, its impact was minimal because Chinese carvings of jadeite predating the late eighteenth century are unknown. In the 1780s the jadeite trade between Burma and China began on a significant scale. Although its beginnings are obscure, in the latter part of the eighteenth century the influx of jadeite into the imperial lapidaries of China was substantial. This influx was possibly the result of the extended domination of the Ch'ing dynasty emperor into Yunnan Province in southwestern China and over the Burmese border into Kachin territory, and the jadeite was a tribute paid to the Chinese emperor. This jadeite jade became known as *new jade* to distinguish it from the well-established nephrite jade of China's Kunlun Mountains (Ng and Root, 1984). This new jade was quickly adopted by the Qing dynasty emperor Qianlong (1736–1796) who preferred the rich, bright colors of jadeite over the more subdued colors of nephrite. By the nineteenth century, jadeite, particularly the rich chromium-green variety known as *imperial jade*, became highly sought after.

Detailed accounts of the mining activity in the Tawmaw area during the late eighteenth and early nineteenth centuries are almost unknown. The first Europeans known to visit the area were a Captain Hannay (1837) and a Dr. Griffith (1847). Both men published their accounts, although Dr. Griffith was the first to note the mining activity. He noted in his 1846 visit that trenches up to 20 feet deep were dug in a boulder conglomerate to recover rounded boulders of jadeite. Interestingly, jadeite jade was not described as a separate species until 1863. Damour (1863, 1881) reported that jadeite was a member of the pyroxene group of minerals, whereas nephrite jade was an amphibole. The in situ deposits of jadeite were not yet known. In 1892 the first geologist to visit the jadeite mines, Noetling (1893), reported on the geology and occurrence of jadeite. His samples were later described by Bauer (1895). Given the hostile terrain and generally primitive conditions, his work was remarkably thorough and today remains the basis for our knowledge of the geology of the area. He noted that in situ jadeite was discovered just 15 years before his March 1892 visit, suggesting a discovery of 1877 for the jadeite-albite dikes. Noetling's work was expanded upon by later visits by Bleeck (1908) and Chhibber (1934a, 1934b). Surprisingly little changed in the area between these visits, except that kero-

sene cans were replaced by mechanized steam pumps to dewater the mines after the rainy season. In more recent years, dynamite and drills have also been introduced. In 1934 Chhibber reported that one large mine designated "Dwingyi" existed at Tawmaw; it consisted of six shafts and numerous tunnels. The shafts were named after the people who dug them. A smaller mine, Kadon dwin, run by C. W. Chater of the Burchin Syndicate, had a 50-foot vertical shaft of the jadeite dike. The industry was declining to 50 or 60 miners by the early 1930s.

General Geology

Of the numerous early geologic studies and mapping of the Hpakan-Tawmaw jade tract (Noetling, 1893; Bauer, 1895; Bleeck, 1908; Lacroix, 1930; Fig. 7-4), the most detailed and important were those of Chhibber (1934a, 1934b) and most recently Soe-Win (1968). Soe-Win (1968) used the work of Chhib-

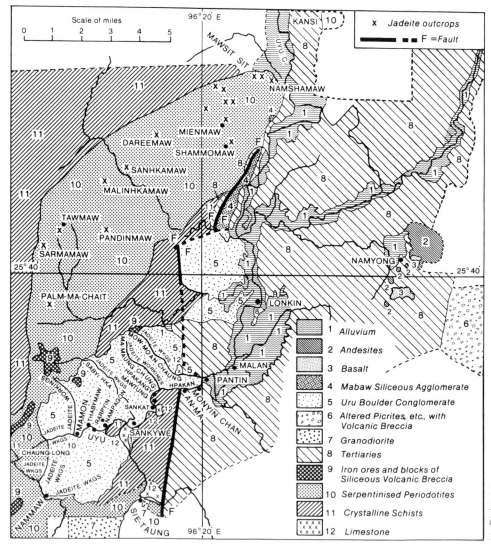

Figure 7-4. Detailed geologic Map of the Tawmaw Jade Mines (adapted from Soe-Win, 1968).

ber (1934a) to apply the geology of the deposit to more effective mining operations. Due to extremely thick jungle and inhospitable conditions, geologic work has been exceedingly difficult. The oldest rocks in the area are the Permian-Carboniferous plateau limestones assigned by Chhibber (1934b), which commonly form bedrock. The plateau limestone is generally crystalline where it has been invaded by plutonic rocks such as granite. In fact, rubies have been reported near such contacts in the Tawmaw area (Bleeck, 1908). The age of the plateau limestone was determined by marker fossils such as Foraminifera. Locally, the limestone has undergone metosomatic replacement, particularly silica replacement. These early studies revealed that the most important rock units of the area, however, consist principally of serpentinized peridotite of late Cretaceous age that have intruded a series of crystalline schists, including chlorite, actinolite, kyanite, graphite, and glaucophane schists. These rocks extend as one continuous mass from the Uru River below Mamon northward above Kansi (Chhibber, 1934a). Typically, these peridotites are dunites that have been partially to totally serpentinized and mantled by a thick horizon of lateritic soil. The crystalline schists are really a continuous series of metamorphic rocks, as noted above. These schists are overlain by sandstones and conglomerates of Tertiary age. The Uru boulder conglomerates, of Pleistocene age, are very important economically, because they contain boulders of jadeite that have weathered out of jadeite albite dikes in the peridotite.

Granite of Tertiary age makes up a large portion of the district, where it forms typically a rolling topography. Chhibber (1934a) considers the granite to be so extensive that it could be considered a batholith. This same igneous event may have given rise to the volcanic rocks in the area, including "altered picrites" (basalts?), andesites, and agglomerates.

Chhibber (1934a) subdivided the Tertiary age sediments into the Hkuma series of Oligocene-Miocene age sandstones interbedded with shale, locally carbonaceous, and the Namting series. The Namting series is Miocene-Pliocene in age and forms great thicknesses of sandstones, shales, and conglomerates. Fossil plant material has been observed in the latter.

Late Tertiary plutonic rocks have also been observed, including minor outcrops of gabbros that intrude the Tertiary sediments, granodiorites, and quartz diorites.

The Uru boulder conglomerate and recent alluvium are discussed in detail later in this chapter.

Occurrence of Jadeite in Burma

Jadeite is principally found at three locations in the Kachin Hills of northern Burma: at Tawmaw, at Hweka, and at Mamon. Each of these three locations exhibits a different mode of occurrence for jadeite. At Tawmaw, by far the most important jadeite occurrence, jadeite and albite occur in situ as dikes within a serpentinized peridotite (Fig. 7-5). Chhibber (1934a) placed the age of these dikes as early Tertiary. At Hweka, jadeite occurs as rounded alluvial boulders in the Pleistocene age Uru conglomerate. In the Mamon area, alluvial jadeite boulders are recovered from the Uru riverbed and from minor tributaries in the area.

A total of four jadeite-albite dikes were described by Chhibber (1934a). These four dikes are parallel to subparallel and extend for a total of approximately 4 miles. These include the Tawmaw dike, which extends in a northeast-southwest direction for a distance of about 300 m; the Mienmaw dike, which runs north-south for approximately 2.5 km; the Pangmaw dike running northwest to southeast for about 1.5 km; and the Namshamaw dike, which is believed to be an extension of the Pangmaw dike. These jadeite-albite dikes consist mostly of these two minerals, but also contain glaucophane, the amphibole actinolite, and typically possess a border zone of soft, green

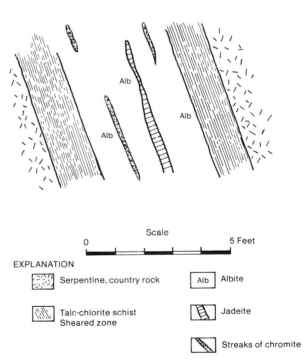

Figure 7-5. *Generalized cross-section of jadeite occurrences near Tawmaw, Burma (adapted from Soe-Win, 1968).*

Figure 7-6. Mining jadeite near Tawmaw, Burma. Photo by Edward Gübelin.

"chlorite" (Bleeck, 1908). Chhibber (1934a) reexamined the border zone and determined the "chlorite" to actually be calcite, jadeite, and "serpentinous" minerals.

The most important alluvial jadeite deposits are found in the Uru boulder conglomerate, possibly Pleistocene; named by Chhibber (1934a) after the river that was responsible for its formation, it ranges in width from 3 km to 6 km maximum at Mamon and may obtain thicknesses exceeding 300 m. Rounded jadeite boulders occur in the conglomerate along with equally rounded boulders of crystalline schists, serpentinite, and rocks representing all the older rock units of the area. Typically, these boulders are poorly cemented by a lateritic clay. According to Soe-Win (1968), a typical cross-section of the Uru boulder conglomerate consists of three horizons resting on bedrock: the basal jadeite-bearing conglomerate overlain by a layer of pebbles and gravel, and a capping of alluvium. Jadeite boulders are also found in the *Tertiaries*, a generalized term for alluvial sandstones.

These deposits are relatively minor in extent and are best observed near the towns of Lonkin, Kansi, and Hweka.

More significant are the recent alluvial deposits of jadeite found in the bed of the Uru River itself. Jadeite is recovered as rounded boulders in the debris of the Uru River for about 15 to 20 miles downstream from the village of Sanka to the Mamon area. This stretch of river flanks Tawmaw Hill, which contains the primary jadeite deposits; no jadeite is found in the river above Sanka, and very little jadeite is recovered below Mamon. All of the small tributaries that feed the Uru, from the plateau that makes up Tawmaw Hill, contain jadeite. These so-called river mines are by far the oldest and contain the finest-quality jadeite (Noetling, 1893). When Bleeck visited the area in 1907, the jadeite recovery was limited in the riverbed to the area around Mamon and the workings as far north as Sanka had been abandoned. Nowadays, the jadeite recovery is centered around Hpakan (Gübelin, personal communication).

Mining Methods

The mining methods in the Tawmaw area are reasonably primitive (Fig. 7-6) and, of course, differ in the recovery of jadeite from the dike versus the alluvium. When a dike was found on the surface, it was followed underground until flooding prevented further development. Prior to the 1930s, buckets or kerosene cans were used to dewater the mines. Since the 1930s, mechanical steam pumps have been employed effectively to allow deeper mine development. Due to jadeite's tremendous toughness, however, chisels and even pneumatic drills are relatively ineffective. The more primitive method of fire setting has been very effective, however. The rock face is heated in this method; when sufficiently hot, it is quickly cooled by splashing water onto the hot rocks. The thermal shock fractures the rocks, which can then be more easily worked with hammer and crowbars.

The alluvial mining from the recent riverbed and older conglomerates consists simply of removing overburden and exposing the basal jadeite-bearing layer in the conglomerate (Fig. 7-7). Accord-

Figure 7-7. Overview of the alluvial mining near Tawmaw, Burma. Photo by Edward Gübelin.

ing to Soe-Win (1968), this is done by simple pit mining, that is, by digging small pits to depths of 6 m or more through very hard ground. When the jadeite-bearing gravel is reached, the boulders are sorted and inspected by hand. During the dry season from December to May, miners commonly mine the recent streambeds themselves. This entails building a dam of bamboo, rock, and earth. The dam is constantly enlarged by the debris from the mining operation. During mining, bamboo hand pumps or diesel pumps are employed to keep the area dewatered. Normally, four or five men work a claim at one time. During the rainy season, ground sluicing in the surrounding hillsides becomes a popular means of mining jadeite. An area of mining is selected and water is then ground sluiced in from a distant source and sprayed on the working area to remove topsoil and conglomerates until bedrock is reached. As the gravels are washed, they are sorted for boulders of

jadeites, and the debris is dumped to the side. Material is then sent to Mogaung for cutting (Fig. 7-8).

Important Jadeite Collections

Identifying a few examples of jadeite as the world's finest is exceedingly difficult. Individual pieces are generally part of large collections that are dominated by the much more common nephrite jade, especially if the collection contains an abundance of pre-eighteenth-century material. Therefore, pointing out the more important collections of Chinese jade is perhaps better, with the assumption that these collections also contain some very fine examples of jadeite.

Saying which one collection is the world's finest is also difficult. Many of China's treasures were looted in the mid-nineteenth century, particularly the 1860 looting of the Summer Palace, and found their way to Europe and the United States, where they remain today. Still, by sheer volume, the finest

Figure 7-8. Cutting large jadeite boulder at Mogaung, Burma. Photo by Edward Gübelin.

Figure 7-9. *One of the finest examples of jadeite is this extraordinary 35-cm-high lavender jadeite vase from the Ch'ing dynasty. It is part of the gem collection of the Smithsonian Institution. Photo by Harold and Erica Van Pelt.*

collection is probably in the National Palace Museum in Taipei, Taiwan.

In Europe, the largest collections of Chinese jade are in the British Museum, the Victoria and Albert Museum, and the Fitzwilliam Museum at Cambridge, and the Bauer Collection in Geneva (Gübelin, personal communication).

The Royal Ontario Museum in Toronto, Canada, has a collection of more than 1,000 pieces of Chinese jade.

In the United States, the Avery Brundage collection of Chinese jade housed in the DeYoung Museum in San Francisco is possibly the most comprehensive jade collection in the world. The Eugene Fuller Memorial Collection in the Seattle Art Museum is also considered to be among the top collections, at least in the United States. Other major collections can be found in the Lizzadro Museum in Oak Park, Illinois; the Bishop Collection in the Metropolitan Museum of Art in New York; the Fogg Art Museum at Harvard in Boston; the John L. and Helen Kellog Hall exhibition in the Field Museum in Chicago; the Nelson Gallery of Art in Kan-

sas City, Missouri; and, finally, the Smithsonian Museum of Natural History, which has a superb collection of 140 pieces donated in 1959 by Edmund C. Monell and also the very important Freer collection.

From these collections and other private collections, a few jadeite pieces do stand out. The Smithsonian Institution has a 14-inch-high jade dragon vase of very fine lavender jade that was donated by Marjorie Merriweather Post (Fig. 7-9). The Crystalite Corporation Collection in Arizona has several very fine examples of jadeite, including a significant necklace of "imperial" green beads (Fig. 7-10) and other significant jadeite carvings (Figs. 7-11 and 7-12). The Natural History Museum of Los Angeles County has a particularly fine imperial jade carving in its Hixon collection (Fig. 7-13).

The Lizzadro Museum of Lapidary Art has several outstanding examples of carved jadeite, including a 14½-inch-high lavender figure of guanyin with yellow bamboo; a 21⅜-inch-high pagoda incense burner; and a 7¼-inch-diameter pair of deep green jadeite bowls.

Figure 7-10. Extraordinary imperial jadeite necklace and earrings from the J. and E. Greenspan collection. Photo by Harold and Erica Van Pelt.

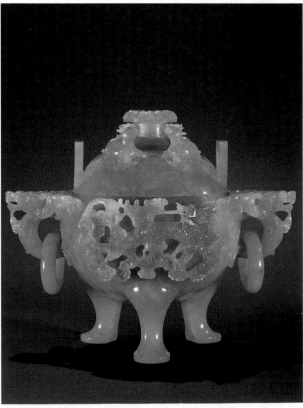

Figure 7-11. A fire-breathing dragon is carved in high relief on this 12-cm-high, late-nineteenth-century jadeite vessel from the J. and E. Greenspan collection. Photo by Harold and Erica Van Pelt.

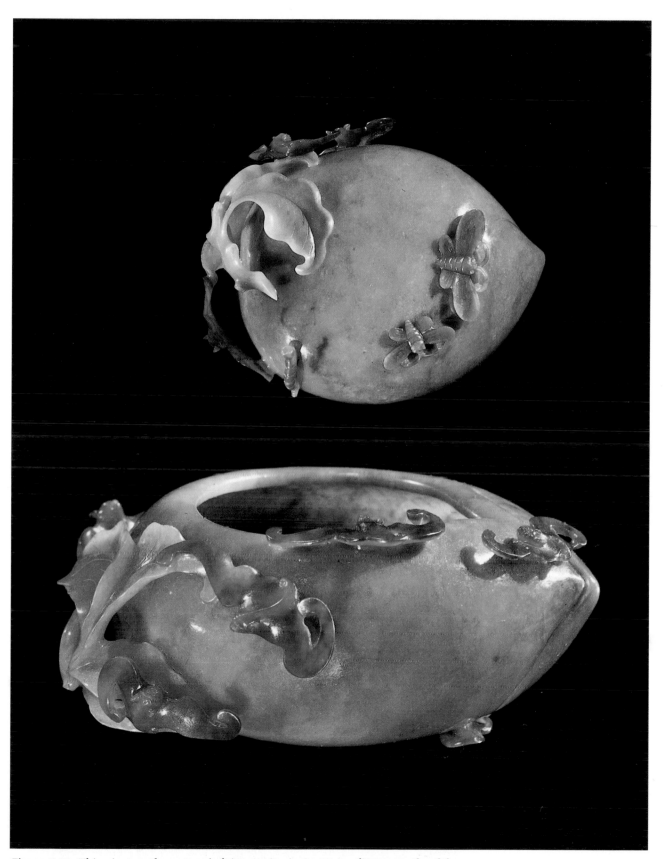

Figure 7-12. *This nineteenth-century jadeite carving is an outstanding example of the Chinese use of color and symbolism in jade. It measures approximately 12.5 by 10 cm. From the J. and E. Greenspan collection. Photo by Harold and Erica Van Pelt.*

Figure 7-13. *The most-sought after variety of jadeite, which was historically reserved for nobility, is rich green imperial jadeite. This particularly fine, approximately 25-carat carving is from the Hixon Collection of the Natural History Museum of Los Angeles County. Photo by Harold and Erica Van Pelt.*

REFERENCES

Bauer, M. 1895. On the jadeite and other rocks from Tawmaw in upper Burma. *Rec. Geol. Surv. India* 28:91–105.

Bleeck, A. W. G. 1908. Jadeite in the Kachin Hills, upper Burma. *Rec. Geol. Surv. India* 36:254–285.

Chhibber, H. L. 1934(a). *The Mineral Resources of Burma.* Macmillan, London.

Chhibber, H. L. 1934(b). *The Geology of Burma.* Macmillan, London.

Chihara, K. 1971. *Mineralogy and Paragenesis of Jadeites from the Omi-Kotaki Area, Central Japan.* Mineral Society of Japan, Tokyo, Special Paper 1.

Damour, A. 1846. Analyse dur Jade oriental reunion de cette substance a la Tremolite. *Ann. Chem. Phys.* 3(16)469–474.

Damour, A. 1863. Notice et analyse sur le jade verte: Reunion de cettes matiere mineral a la famille wernerites. *Comptes Rendus* 56:861–865.

Damour, A. 1891. Nouvelles analyses sur la jadeite et sur quelques roches sodiferes. *Bulletin Societe Mineralogique de France* 4:156–160.

DeRoever, W. F. 1955. Genesis of jadeite by low grade metamorphism. *American Journal of Science* 253:283–298.

Desautels, P. E. 1986. *The Jade Kingdom.* Van Nostrand Reinhold Company, New York. 118 pages.

Foshag, W. F. 1957. *Mineralogical Studies in Guatemalan Jade.* U.S. National Museum Publication 4307. U.S. National Museum, Washington, D.C.

Foshag, W. F., and R. Leslie. 1955. Jadeite from Manzanal, Guatemala. *American Antiquity* 21:81–83.

Griffith. 1847. *Journal of Travel in Assam, Burma.* Butan, etc. Calcutta, 132.

Gübelin, E. 1965. Jade albit—ein neuer Schmuckstein aus Burma. *Zt. dt. Gemmol. Ges. Heft.* 51:4–22.

Gübelin, E. 1976. Jadeite, der grüne Schatz aus Burma. *Lapis* 3(2):17–28.

Hannay, C. 1837. *Journal of the Asiatic Soc. of Bengal* 6:265.

Iwao, S. 1953. Albitite and associated jadeite rock from Kataki District Japan: A study in ceramic raw material. *Report of the Geological Survey of Japan 153.*

Keverne, R. 1975. Jade: A review of the exhibition at the Victoria and Albert Museum, London. *Arts of Asia* 5(4).

Lacroix, A. 1930. La jadeite de Bermanie: Les roches qu'elle constitute ou qui l'accompagnent: Composition et origine. *Bulletin Societe Mineralogique France* 53.

McBirney, A. R., et al. 1967. Eclogites and jadeites from the Motagua fault zone, Guatemala. *American Mineralogist* 52:908–918.

Meen, V. B. 1962. Jade in Burma. *Lapidary Journal* 816–835.

Ng, J., and E. Root. 1984. *Jade for You: Value Guide to Fine Jewelry Jade.* Jade and Gem Corp. of America. 107 pages.

Noetling, F. 1893. Note on the occurrence of jadeite in the Union of Burma. *Rec. Geol. Survey of India* 26:26–31.

Scalisi, P., and D. Cook. 1983. *Classic Mineral Localities of the World: Asia and Australia.* Van Nostrand Reinhold Company, New York. 226 pages.

Soe-Win, U. 1968. The application of geology to the mining of jade. *Union of Burma J. Sci. and Tech.* 1:445–446.

Turner, F. 1981. *Metamorphic Petrology: Mineralogical, Field, and Tectonic Aspects.* McGraw-Hill Book Company, New York. 524 pages.

PART IV

Gemstones Formed at Great Depths

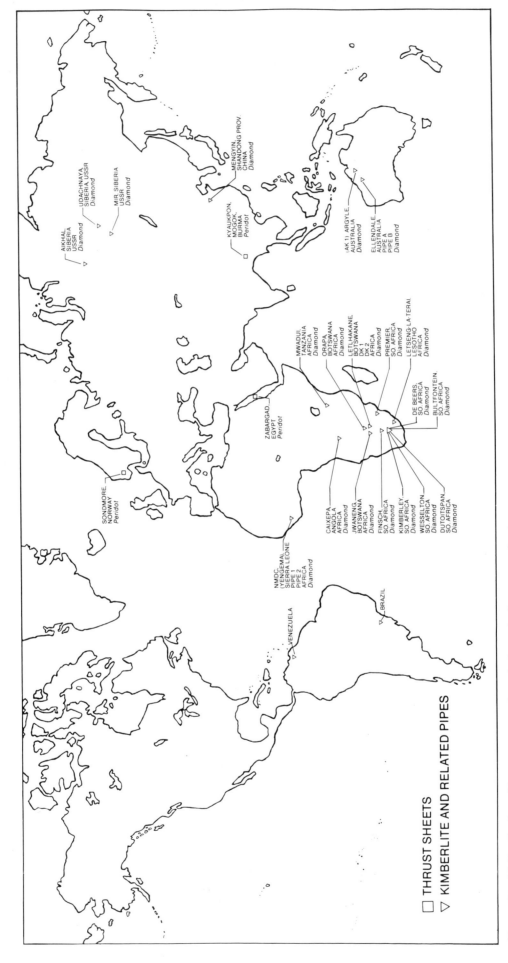

AIKHAL
SIBERIA
USSR
Diamond

UDACHNAYA
SIBERIA, USSR
Diamond

MIR, SIBERIA
USSR
Diamond

MENGYIN,
SHANDONG PROV.
CHINA
Diamond

KYAUKPON,
MOGOK,
BURMA
Peridot

(AK 1) ARGYLE,
AUSTRALIA
Diamond

ELLENDALE
AUSTRALIA
PIPE A
PIPE B
Diamond

MWADUI,
TANZANIA
AFRICA
Diamond

ORAPA,
BOTSWANA
AFRICA
Diamond

LETLHAKANE
BOTSWANA
DK 1
DK 2
AFRICA
Diamond

PREMIER,
SO. AFRICA
Diamond

LETSENG-LA-TERAI,
LESOTHO
AFRICA
Diamond

DE BEERS,
SO. AFRICA
Diamond

BULTFONTEIN,
SO. AFRICA
Diamond

ZABARGAD,
EGYPT
Peridot

SONDMORE,
NORWAY
Peridot

CAIXEPA,
ANGOLA
AFRICA
Diamond

JWANENG,
BOTSWANA
AFRICA
Diamond

FINSCH,
SO. AFRICA
Diamond

KIMBERLEY
SO. AFRICA
Diamond

WESSELTON,
SO. AFRICA
Diamond

DUTOITSPAN,
SO. AFRICA
Diamond

NMDC,
(YENGEMA)
SIERRA LEONE
PIPE 1
PIPE 2
AFRICA
Diamond

BRAZIL

VENEZUELA

□ THRUST SHEETS
▽ KIMBERLITE AND RELATED PIPES

Map 4. World distribution of important gem deposits brought from great depths.

116

All the gemstones that we have considered thus far form within the earth's crust—the planet's thin outer shell. Two important gemstones, peridot and diamond, form in the very thick layer of rock, called the mantle, *between the crust of the earth and its metallic core. The mantle makes up 83 percent of our planet's volume, but rarely do pieces of it reach the surface.*

Compressive forces acting on areas where the earth's crust is thin may produce thrust sheets, where a slice of the earth's crust and portions of the underlying mantle are forced over the top of the adjoining crust. Subsequent erosion will in time reveal the overthrust mantle rock, but only samples of the uppermost part of the mantle, from depths between 6 and 20 miles, are exposed in this way. One of the most important constituents of this part of the mantle is forsterite olivine, which is known as peridot when it is of gem quality.

The finest peridot in the world comes from Zabargad (formerly St. John's Island), a tiny island in the Red Sea that is situated on a thrust sheet. Despite the desolate nature of this island and its lack of fresh water, peridot has drawn people here for thousands of years. Small pits and tunnels, some hundreds of years old, dot the island. Peridot has not been mined commercially on the island since before World War II, however. The political instability of the region, high cost of mining, and the availability of peridot from more accessible and hospitable places in the world continue to discourage modern mining undertakings there.

Diamonds reach the earth's surface in turbulent, volcanic eruptions that originate in the mantle at depths between 90 and 200 miles. No known eruption of this type has occurred in recorded history.

Nevertheless, geologic clues provide a good picture of their nature.

Diamond-bearing deposits are most commonly composed of a rare rock, kimberlite, or of kimberlitelike rocks like lamproites, which contain broken and somewhat rounded fragments of solid rock from both the mantle and the crust. The deposits are in the form of narrow vertical tubes called pipes, which flare out into a cone shape near the surface and may be as much as several thousand feet across.

Although the origin of kimberlite deposits is still open to debate, most scientists believe that they originated from gases and liquids under high pressure in the mantle. These highly fluid magmas rose at great speed along weaknesses in the crust and violently tumbled pieces of rocks they picked up along the way, until they burst explosively through the surface. Diamonds are often found as single crystals embedded in the volcanic kimberlite matrix.

The study of kimberlites as sources of diamond is relatively recent. Until 1870, diamond had been found only in alluvial deposits. In that year, the first of several diamond pipes was discovered near the town of Kimberley in South Africa (hence the name kimberlite). Since this time kimberlite deposits have been found in many parts of the world, including most of western and southern Africa, many areas of northern Siberia, China, and, most importantly, in Western Australia. In 1979 diamonds were discovered in the Kimberley area of Western Australia. Today, that area is the number one producer in the world, with an average output of 30 million carats annually (Map 4).

8

Mantle Thrust Sheet Gem Deposits:
The Zabargad Island, Egypt, Peridot Deposits

Gemstones formed at great depth, in the earth's mantle, can be studied and recovered only when this mantle material is brought to the earth's surface through one of a number of geologic processes. Corundum, such as the rubies from the Chanthaburi-Trat area of Thailand, may be formed in the mantle and brought to the surface as basaltic volcanic eruptions. Diamonds are exclusively brought from great depths in the mantle through unique types of volcanoes known as *pipes*. Where the earth's crust thins due to rifting, mantle material, including peridot, may be thrust to the surface in sheets (Fig. 8-1).

In some areas of the earth's surface, forces pull the earth's crust apart and cause it to become thin and fractured. This is known as *rifting*. If these forces reverse, the crust may be pushed back to-

gether, thrusting one side over the other. Portions of the mantle just beneath the crust may be carried along with the overriding crust and thereby reach the surface as mantle thrust sheets. Thrust sheets originate at depths between 6 and 20 miles below the surface with temperatures between 800° and 1,000°C.

Peridot, the gem variety of forsterite olivine, is usually found in the mantle only as small crystals. Sometimes, during the upward movement of mantle thrust sheets, hot fluids dissolve the mantle-formed crystals and redeposit them as larger, gem-quality crystals.

In spite of its small size, Zabargad Island is an extraordinary source of information for geologists seeking evidence of the early rifting history of the Red Sea and the nature of its underlying mantle.

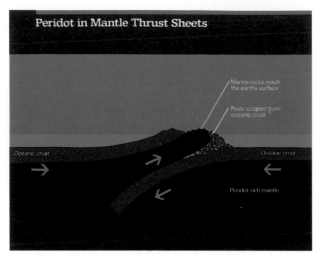

Figure 8-1. Diagram showing emplacement of mantle thrust sheet. Courtesy of the Natural History Museum of Los Angeles County.

Figure 8-2. Faceted peridot from Zabargad, Egypt. This stone is part of the Phillips Collection of the Natural History Museum of Los Angeles County. Photo by Harold and Erica Van Pelt.

From a gemologist's point of view, the island has historically provided the world with its finest specimens of gem olivine, or peridot (Fig. 8-2).

THE ZABARGAD ISLAND, EGYPT, PERIDOT DEPOSITS

The Red Sea is one of the most dynamic tectonic features on the earth's surface. Geologists view the Red Sea as an embryonic ocean.

The Red Sea forms part of a rift system that includes the Gulf of Aden and the East African rift in the south, and the Gulf of Suez and the Gulf of Aqaba in the north. Rifting initiated in the late Oligocene-Miocene time.

The northern Red Sea is a continental rift that has developed nearly to the point where sea floor spreading initiates. Active sea floor spreading is occurring in the southern end of the Red Sea.

Zabargad has yielded information on the nature of the upper mantle in a young rift zone with lithosphere transitional from continental to oceanic. Studies of the peridotite suggest an origin of more than 30-km depth.

The peridotites were probably uplifted in connection with the development of the Red Sea rift.

The island of Zabargad is probably a tectonically uplifted fragment of Red Sea lithosphere that has exposed blocks of mantle-derived peridotite. The peridotites on the island, which are unusually fresh and free of serpentinization, were studied in detail by Bonatti and associates (1981) following field trips to the island in 1979 and 1980.

Location and Access

Zabargad Island is located in the northern Red Sea, approximately 54 km southeast of the tip of the Ra's Banās peninsula and 50 km east of the port of Berenice. Its precise location is latitude 23°36'16" north and longitude 36°11'42" east. The triangular island is about 3 km on a side or less than 5 square km in size. The highest point, approximately 235 m, on this desolate island is Peridot Hill, the southern of three peridotite masses on the island (Fig. 8-3).

Access to the island is only by boat, as the island has no airstrip. An interesting description of the 7-hour journey by boat from the port of Ra's Banās is found in Bancroft (1984).

History

Zabargad Island has produced the world's finest peridot for possibly 3,500 years, since the mines were worked on behalf of the Egyptian pharaohs as early as 1500 B.C. According to Wilson (1976), peridot that could have come only from Zabargad has been found in archaeological excavations in Alexandria, Egypt. Pliny the Elder (23–79 A.D.) noted that the Greeks called the island Topazos, from which the ancient name for peridot, *topazion*, was derived. During its early history, the island was also called the Serpent Isle. During the Crusades, Westerners discovered the island and named it St. John's, a name retained today by some gemologists. Then the island was lost for many hundreds of years until it was rediscovered as a source for peridot in the early part of the twentieth century.

Figure 8-3. View of Peridot Hill, the highest point on the island (235 m above sea level), as seen from the sea. Photo by Peter Bancroft.

Its first mention in modern times is noted by Bauer (1904), who gave only vague reference to the location for fine peridot showing up on the European market. The first specific mention of St. John's Island as a source for fine peridot was made by Michel (1906). During the twentieth century, St. John's Island has been cited as Zeberget, Zebirged, and Zabargad. The latter, meaning *peridot* in Arabic, is the most commonly used name today.

Living conditions and mining activity on Zabargad have always been exceedingly difficult. It is truly a desert island with virtually no fresh water and only meager desert vegetation. Little, if anything, is known about mining activity prior to this century, except that it has always been very primitive—simple digging of tunnels along exposed veins until the veins pinched out or the tunnels were no longer safe (Fig. 8-4). In the twentieth century, mining activity reached its peak between 1906 and World War I. During this time, mining rights were held solely in the hands of the Khedive, the Turkish Viceroy in Egypt (Gübelin, 1981). In 1922, the Egyptian government gave the mining rights to

Figure 8-4. Main gem pits near bottom of Peridot Hill on Zabargad Island. Photo by Peter Bancroft.

Figure 8-5. Ruins of mining camp on Zabargad built in the early twentieth century. Peridot Hill is in the background. Photo by Peter Bancroft.

Figure 8-6. View of old peridot waste dumps on the eastern flank of Peridot Hill. Photo by Peter Bancroft.

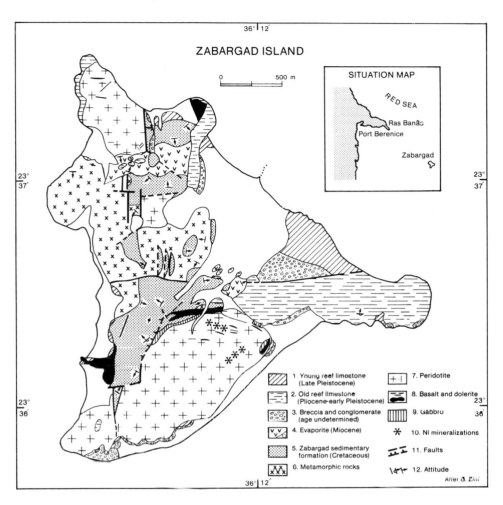

ZABARGAD ISLAND

0   500 m

SITUATION MAP

RED SEA

Ras Banãs
Port Berenice

Zabargad

1. Young reef limestone (Late Pleistocene)
2. Old reef limestone (Pliocene-early Pleistocene)
3. Breccia and conglomerate (age undetermined)
4. Evaporite (Miocene)
5. Zabargad sedimentary formation (Cretaceous)
6. Metamorphic rocks
7. Peridotite
8. Basalt and dolerite
9. Gabbro
10. Ni mineralizations
11. Faults
12. Attitude

After G. Zini

Figure 8-7. Geologic map of the island of Zabargad. Inset shows the relationship of the island to the Egyptian mainland (Adapted from Bonatti et al., 1981).

the Red Sea Mining Company. This company began mining in 1924 and introduced relatively modern facilities to the island. The ruins of these facilities are still visible to visitors to the island today (Fig. 8-5). Miners commonly sieved the crystals from the ore and left dumps of concentrate over the flanks of Peridot Hill (Fig. 8-6). The Red Sea Mining Company was very successful in supplying fine gem peridot to cutters in France until the outbreak of World War II. After World War II, mining activity was sporadic, and all but ceased when the mines were nationalized by the Egyptian government in 1958. A detailed account of the history of peridot mining on Zabargad is given in Gübelin (1981).

Geology

Zabargad is important not only to gemologists but also to geologists interested in the Red Sea area. The first geological reconnaissance mapping of Zabargad was completed by Moon (1923). His work was the cornerstone of all that was known of Zabargad's geology until interest in the Red Sea's role in plate tectonics theory sparked a great deal of

work on the island's geology in the 1970s and 1980s. Today, this island is one of the most thoroughly studied 5 square km known. El Shazly and associates (1972, 1974) studied details of the mineralogy of the island. Modern detailed geologic mapping by Bonatti and co-workers (1981) marked the beginning of intensive work on all aspects of the island's geologic history (Fig. 8-7). Petrological and geochemical studies of the peridotites were done by Bonatti and associates (1983, 1986, 1987), and structural work on the island was accomplished by Nicolas and Boudier (1987). In 1988 a major series of papers on all aspects of the island was published (Seyler and Bonatti, 1988; Piccardo et al., 1988; Petrini et al., 1988).

The island is generally thought to be a tectonically uplifted fragment of the Red Sea lithosphere exposing blocks of mantle-derived peridotite. Zabargad lies in a zone of transition between the southern Red Sea, with a nearly continuous axial rift valley carpeted by an oceanic type of crust, and the Northern Red Sea, where an axial rift valley is poorly developed or absent. Nicolas and Boudier (1987) concluded that Zabargad Island resulted from mantle diapirism contemporaneous with early rifting of the Red Sea. Styles and Gardes (1983) believe that the diapir may be part of a much larger dome that may extend to a depth of at least 8 km.

The basement of Zabargad Island is composed of fresh plagioclase-spinel lherzolites (peridotites). These mantle-derived peridotites are in contact with metamorphic amphibolites and felsitic gneisses. The peridotites and metamorphic rocks are overlain by the Zabargad formation, a suite of shales, quartzites, and limestones. The Zabargad formation is unconformably overlain by the gently folded evaporite unit, the old reef limestone, and young reef limestone (Bonatti et al., 1981). The evaporite unit is middle Miocene in age and occurs discordantly in a syncline of the Zabargad formation. It has been mildly folded. The old reef and young reef limestones are both Pleistocene in age and confined to the eastern extreme of the island.

The peridotites are found in three areas of Zabargad, each of which forms a structural high on the island. The northern and central peridotites are considered spinel lherzolites, and the southern peridotite is a plagioclase lherzolite. The southern peridotite, known as Peridot Hill, is by far the largest of the peridotite bodies. Located along the southwestern shore of the island, it is bounded to the north by a major fault zone, which may have significance for the genesis of gem peridot. Here, the peridotite is uncharacteristically strongly serpentinized, and the hydrothermal alteration also gave rise to gem peridot (Bonatti et al., 1981). Nicolas and Boudier (1988) determined an age for the peridotite mantle diapir emplacement as late Oligocene or Miocene and confirm that it is related to the initial opening of the Red Sea.

The metamorphic rocks on Zabargad Island consist of amphibolites interlayered with felsitic gneisses. These metamorphic rocks are in contact with the mantle-derived peridotites (Seyler and Bonatti, 1988). Nicolas and Boudier (1987) concluded that the metamorphic rocks are probably related to the intrusion of the mantle diapir into the crust, but the exact origin of the gneisses could not be determined (Boudier et al., 1988). The age of the metamorphics could not be accurately determined due to excess argon (Villa, 1988).

Numerous diabase dikes crosscut the peridotite and gneisses. Diabase sills are particularly well developed along the contact between the peridotites and the Zabargad formation. These diabase intrusions belong to two distinct generations: First, diabase dikes up to 1 m wide intruded the metamorphic rocks and the peridotites; and second, the diabase dikes, mainly in the southern peridotite (Peridot Hill), and related diabase sills up to several tens of meters thick (Petrini et al., 1988). Villa (1988)

determined the age of dike emplacement at less than 20 million years, about the same age as the peridotite uplift and the initial opening of the Red Sea.

Peridot Occurrence

Generally, gem peridot occurrences on Zabargad Island are limited to the eastern slope of the southern peridotite, the 235-m-high Peridot Hill. In the vicinity of the major east-west fault zone, gem peridot crystals occur in veins that transverse the highly serpentinized peridotite. These veins consist nearly entirely of olivine, with minor nickle-rich serpentine and iron-nickle oxides. The gem peridot is found in open cavities in the veins and as overgrowths on flat brown olivine crystals that are up to 20 cm long (Kurat et al., 1982a). Few of the crystals are found attached to vug walls. Most are found in the rubble at the bottom of the vugs. The gem crystals are typically pristine with little or no etching, unlike the heavily etched crystals from the only other source of peridot crystals, Burma. The Zabargad crystals are typically flattened and tabular in form (Fig. 8-8).

According to Clochiatti and associates (1981), the peridot crystals can be attributed to the hydrothermal alteration that heavily serpentinized the southern peridotite. This alteration took place along north-northwest to south-southeast veins at temperatures of about 750° to 950°C and near surface pressures. Clochiatti and associates (1981) postulate that the alteration and peridot mineralization was the result of seawater contamination during the final stages of the mantle intrusion, when the peridotite penetrated the seafloor (Kurat et al., 1982a). During the final stages of emplacement, seawater invaded fractures in the peridotite, resulting in metasomatic mineralization and forming the gem peridot. Piccardo and associates (1988) suggest that this mineralization was then followed by the emplacement of the diabase dikes and final emplacement on the seafloor. Clochiatti and co-workers (1981) suggest that the seawater contamination is reflected in the hypersaline fluid inclusions typical of Zabargad peridot.

Important Peridots

Very few important peridots that can definitely be attributed to Zabargad are known today. However, many historical stones can be attributed to the island because of their age. Furthermore, important collections in Europe, including the Treasury of the Three Magi in Cologne and the Vatican, contain peridots mistakenly identified as emerald. Faceted peridots in major museums are commonly of dubious origin. Those possibly from Burma include a 310-carat stone in the Smithsonian Institution, a 192-carat peridot in the Diamond Treasury of the Kremlin in Moscow, several large gems in the Royal Ontario Museum in Toronto, and a 136-carat peridot in the Geological Museum in London.

Zabargad peridots can be distinguished from Burmese by their inclusions. The Zabargad peridot typically contains chromite crystals and abundant fluid inclusions, whereas the Burmese peridot lacks fluid inclusions and typically contains unusual "rectangular" brown biotite flakes.

Important peridot crystals are as rare as their faceted counterparts. According to Bancroft (1984), the largest Zabargad Island crystal was found sometime after 1922 and measured 6.6 by 5.1 by 2.5 cm and was a well-formed, nearly perfect crystal. Fortunately, it was not faceted. It was purchased by the British Museum of Natural History for $100 and can be seen there today (Fig. 8-9). The nearby Geological Museum has a crystal measuring 4.5 by 3.5 cm from Zabargad, and the Montgomery Collection of the Smithsonian Institution includes a major Zabargad peridot crystal. These crystals are differentiated from the characteristically etched Burmese crystals by their pristine condition. Very fine peridot is more commonly found in jewelry as illustrated in Figure 8-10.

Figure 8-8. Peridot crystal from Zabargad from the Montgomery Collection of the Smithsonian Institution. Photo by Rock Currier.

Figure 8-9. Very fine peridot crystal from Zabargad Island, measuring 4 cm in length. Collection of the American Museum of Natural History. Photo by Harold and Erica Van Pelt.

Figure 8-10. One of the finest faceted examples of peridot from Zabargad is this 63.80 carat stone set as a pendant. Photo by Harold and Erica Van Pelt.

REFERENCES

Bancroft, P. 1984. *Gem and Crystal Treasures*. Western Enterprises–Mineralogical Record, Fallbrook, Cal. 488 pages.

Bauer, M. 1904. *Precious Stones*. Charles Griffin and Co., London, 404–407.

Bonatti, E., R. Clochiatti, P. Colantoni, R. Gelmini, G. Marinelli, G. Ottonello, R. Santacroce, M. Taviani, A. A. Abdel-Meguid, H. S. Assaf, and M. A. El Tahir. 1983. Zabargad (St. John's) Island: An uplifted fragment of sub-Red Sea lithosphere. *J. Geol. Soc.* (London) 140:677–690.

Bonatti, E., P. R. Hamlyn, and G. Ottonello. 1981. The upper mantle beneath a young oceanic rift: Peridotites from the island of Zabargad (Red Sea). *Geology* 9:474–491.

Bonatti, E., G. Ottonello, and P. R. Hamlyn. 1986. Peridotites from the island of Zabargad (St. John's) Red Sea: Petrology and geochemistry. *J. Geophys. Res.* 21:599–631.

Bonatti, E., and M. Seyler. 1987. Crustal underplating and evolution in the Red Sea rift: Uplifted gabbro/gneiss crustal complexes on Zabargad and Brothers Islands. *J. Geophys. Res.* 92:12803–12821.

Boudier, F., A. Nicolas, S. Ji, J. R. Kienast, and C. Mevel. 1988. The gneisses of Zabargad Island: Deep crust of a rift. *Tectonophysics* 150:209–277.

Clochiatti, R., D. Massare, and C. Jehanno. 1981. Origine hydrothermale des olivines gemmes de l'ile de Zabargad (St. John), Mer Rouge, par l'etudo de leurs inclusions. *Bull. Mineral* 104:354–360.

El Shazly, E. M., and G. S. Saleeb. 1972. Scapolite-cancrinite mineral association in St. John's Island, Egypt. *24th International Geological Congress (Montreal) Reports* 14:192–199.

El Shazly, E. M., G. S. Saleeb, and N. Zake. 1974. Quaternary basalt in St. John's Island, Red Sea, Egypt. *Egyptian Journal of Geology* 18:137–148.

Gübelin, E. 1981. Zabargad: The ancient peridot island in the Red Sea. *Gems & Gemology* 17:2–8.

Kurat, G., G. Niedermayr, and M. Prinz. 1982a. Peridot von Zabargad, Rotes Meer. *Aufscluss* 33:169–182.

Kurat, G., G. Niedermayr, M. Prinz, and F. Brandstatter. 1982b. High temperature peridotite intrusion into an evaporite sequence, Zabargad, Egypt. *Terra Cognita* 2:240.

Michel, L. 1906. Sur le gisement de chrysolite de l'ile Saint Jean (Mer Rouge). *Bull. Soc. Franc. Min.* 29:360–361.

Moon, F. W. 1923. *Preliminary Geological Report on Saint John's Island (Red Sea)*. Geological Survey of Egypt. Cairo, 36 pages.

Nicolas, A., and F. Boudier. 1987. Structure of Zabargad Island and early rifting of the Red Sea. *J. Geophys. Res.* 92:461–474.

Petrini, R., J. L. Joron, G. Ottonello, E. Bonatti, and M. Seyler. 1988. Basaltic dykes from Zabargad Island, Red Sea: Petrology and Geochemistry. *Tectonophysics* 150:229–248.

Piccardo, G. B., B. Messiga, and R. Vannucci. 1988. The Zabargad peridotite-pyroxenite association: Petrologic constraints to the evolutive history. *Tectonophysics* 150:135–162.

Seyler, M., and E. Bonatti. 1988. Petrology of a gneiss/amphibolite lower crust unit from Zabargad Island. *Tectonophysics* 150:177–207.

Styles, P., and K. Gardes. 1983. St. John's Island (Red Sea): A new geophysical model and its implications for the emplacement of ultraunafic rocks in fracture zones and at continental margins. *Earth Planet. Sci. Lett.* 65:353–368.

Villa, I. M. 1988. [40]Ar/[39]Ar analysis of amphiboles from Zabargad Island (Red Sea). *Tectonophysics* 150:249.

Wilson, W. E. 1976. Saint John's Island, Egypt. *Min. Record* 7:310–314.

9

Diamond Pipes:
The Diamond Deposits of Argyle, Western Australia

One of the few windows through the earth's relatively thin crust into its underlying mantle is the diatreme or pipe that occasionally has pierced the crust to bring mantle material such as diamond to the surface (Fig. 9-1). Experimental work has shown that most synthetic diamonds generally must have very high temperatures (2,000°C) and pressures (70,000 kg/cm²) to form. In nature these conditions exist only at depths of at least 200 km below the earth's surface. Material formed at these depths comes to the surface in pipes, which may be thought of as a very special type of volcano that taps depths as great as 350 km below the earth's surface. The volcanic rock type found in these pipes is called *kimberlite*, named for its type area of Kimberley, South Africa. Since its discovery in 1871, the Kimberley area has yielded more than 200 million carats of diamond and a wealth of geologic information about kimberlite pipes and the earth's upper mantle.

The definition of *kimberlite* has been confusing. Early definitions simply stated that a kimberlite consisted of mafic igneous rock containing mantle phases, commonly including diamond, and occurring as pipes or dikes. Today the definition is far more complex, including mineralogical, chemical, and textural considerations (Guilbert and Park, 1986). Skinner and Clement (1979) proposed the mineralogical and chemical constraints, and Clement et al., (1979) the textural. Mineralogically, kimberlite is a volatile-rich, potassic, ultramafic, igneous rock composed principally of olivine with lesser amounts of phlogopite, diopside, serpentine, or calcite. Other high-pressure, mantle-derived minerals that may be present include chromite, ilmenite, pyrope-garnet, and magnetite. The term *kimberlite* is used to describe a wide range of alkaline ultrabasic rocks that share features typical of the classic kimberlite of the Kimberley region of South Africa. These consist of a diatreme form of

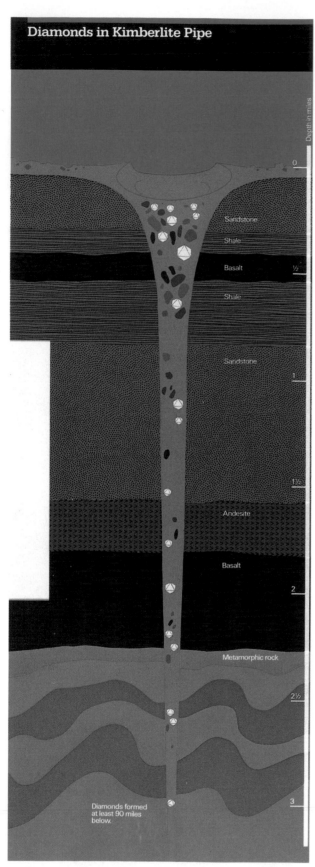

Diamonds in Kimberlite Pipe

Sandstone
Shale
Basalt
Shale
Sandstone
Andesite
Basalt
Metamorphic rock

Depth in miles

0
½
1
1½
2
2½
3

Diamonds formed
at least 90 miles
below.

Figure 9-1. Diagram showing idealized diamond pipe. Courtesy of the Natural History Museum of Los Angeles County.

emplacement and evidence of derivation from the deeper part of the earth's upper mantle; that is, some kimberlites contain garnet lherzolite xenoliths and/or pyrope (Jaques et al., 1984).

The structure and mode of emplacement of these very different igneous structures has been studied in detail over the last few decades. The kimberlite pipes are typically carrot shaped, and Hawthorne (1975) developed a diagrammatic model of a kimberlite pipe shortly after emplacement. Kennedy and Nordlie (1968) noted that these carrot-shaped intrusions became narrower with depth and, in fact, may become dikelike at deeper levels in the crust.

The mode of emplacement has been the subject of great speculation for many years. Traditionally, kimberlite pipes were thought to have been emplaced as very violent, rapid eruptions of mantle material exploding at the surface to form a conelike depression filled with not only volcanic material but also any rock type encountered on its upward journey. It was generally believed that expansion of CO-CO_2-H_2O gases might have chilled the kimberlite during eruption and metastably preserved diamond that ordinarily would burn at the high temperatures found in the lava (Guilbert and Park, 1986).

Kimberlite emplacement theories have recently been revised to suggest that the kimberlites did indeed rise rapidly as magma wedges, but only at depths of 100 to 200 km. Once the surface was approached, magma stoping became important as the emplacement process slowed dramatically. Just below the earth's surface, a "gas cap" formed, exploding and throwing material upward to form a conical crater filled with explosive breccia and tuffs (Guilbert and Park, 1986). Hawthorne (1975) believes that the kimberlite pipe may be shaped like a teardrop rather than a carrot and may pinch out at depth. These "emplacements" commonly occurred as a series of intrusive events that left behind clusters of kimberlite pipes and dikes.

Within an ideal kimberlite pipe, three different forms of kimberlite may be recognized according to a textural classification proposed by Clement and Skinner (1979). These include the hypabyssal, diatreme, and crater kimberlite facies. The hypabyssal facies represents the crystallized, deeper-seated, porphyritic kimberlite. It represents the kimberlitic magma that crystallized below the diatreme. The diatreme facies contains both mantle- and crustal-derived rock fragments with kimberlite lapilli and tuffs in the upper portions. The diatreme facies represents the main mass of the intrusive body. The third kimberlite type found in a pipe is the crater facies. It represents the pyroclastic debris that has fallen back into the crater following the explosive eruption. It may or may not be water laid.

Diamond deposits represent the poorest concentration of any ore deposit known. According to Guilbert and Park (1986), the open-pit mine at Koffiefontein, located approximately 80 km southeast of Kimberley, mines ore yielding about 10 carats of diamond per 100 metric tons of ore. Of this, only about 35 percent is gem quality; the remainder is industrial grade.

Today, kimberlites and related mantle-derived kimberlitelike rocks have been discovered and studied on virtually every continent except Antarctica. Furthermore, many intrusive ultramafic rocks that had previously been dismissed as not kimberlitic and therefore not diamond bearing are being reexamined and found to be indeed diamondiferous. One of the principal factors in this new look at previously dismissed rocks is the recent discovery of diamonds in lamproite intrusions rather than kimberlite intrusions in the Kimberley area in the north of Western Australia. In fact, the Argyle lamproite pipe produced almost 30 million carats of diamonds in its first year of production, making it the largest single producer of diamonds in the world.

Worldwide, about 20 other pipes are significant. The geographic distribution of these pipes is very interesting. All are located in very stable, old, continental shields. These include significant clusters in the Siberian area of the Soviet Union and in many widely distributed areas of the African shield; the eastern margin of the South American shield contains abundant alluvial deposits of diamonds whose parentage was obviously from nearby pipes that have either eroded away or simply not yet been discovered. Kimberlites and kimberlitelike rocks, some of which contain diamonds, are known all the way across the North American continent. The Murfreesboro, Arkansas, lamproite pipe is well known. More recently discovered and far less known is the area around the Colorado-Wyoming border where diamonds have also been discovered in kimberlites.

Argyle Pipe, Western Australia

The richest diamond pipe in the world today is the Argyle (AK1) pipe of the Kimberley region of West Australia, which has been in production only since 1986 (Fig. 9-2). In that year, it produced almost 30 million carats of diamonds. Although Argyle produces some very fine pink diamonds (Fig. 9-3), un-

Figure 9-2. Overview of the Argyle operation in Western Australia. Note mine in the background. Photo by Brian Stevenson. Courtesy of Argyle Diamond Sales.

Figure 9-3. The Argyle pipe is best known for its rare and spectacular pink diamonds. One of the finest recovered to date is this cushion-cut, 2.21-carat, intense pink diamond. Photo by Brian Stevenson. Courtesy of Argyle Diamond Sales.

fortunately, only about 5 percent of the mine output is considered to be of gem quality. However, Argyle is significant for more than its impressive diamond production. It is also significant because it has dramatically altered geologists' perception that diamonds are always related to kimberlites. Even though Argyle was assumed to be a kimberlite when first discovered and given the designation AK1 (Argyle Kimberlite 1), geologists now know that Argyle is an ultrapotassic mantle-derived rock known as *lamproite*. Lamproites have in the past been assumed not to contain diamonds and have therefore been generally overlooked by diamond prospectors. A detailed account of the Argyle pipe and its discovery can be found in Atkinson and associates (1984a, 1984b), Atkinson (1987), Geach (1986), and Fumey (1985).

Location and Access

The Argyle pipe is in the East Kimberley Province of Western Australia (Fig. 9-4), approximately 2,200 km northeast of Perth in a vast area that boasts only five towns with a total population of about 16,000 people. The Argyle pipe occupies a small valley floor near the eastern end of the Matsu Range near the headwaters of Smoke Creek. The valley is the result of preferential weathering of the relatively soft lamproite, which erodes faster than the surrounding sandstone and quartzite walls that form the rim of the valley. The Argyle pipe is named after the nearby 720-square-km, man-made Lake Argyle. As noted above, the pipe was originally given the acronym AK1 for Argyle Kimberlite Number 1. Subsequently, the pipe was determined to be a lamproite, not a kimberlite. The pipe is now simply called the Argyle pipe, and the mine that exploits the pipe is the Argyle mine.

Access to the 450,000-square-km Kimberley region is gained by the all-weather Great Northern Highway, which crosses the area from north to south. As in many rural areas of the world, the secondary roads leading off the main highway are of variable quality but give reasonable access to most areas. With the exception of the Great Northern Highway, all roads are generally impassable during the rainy season, which extends from December through March. Most exploration activities have been carried out using helicopters. Since the Argyle mine has gone into production, the mine can be reached by an all-weather road from the Great Northern Highway, except that access is strictly limited due to security arrangements. Visiting the area requires first gaining permission from the Argyle Diamond Mines Pty. Limited (ADM), who manage and operate the mine.

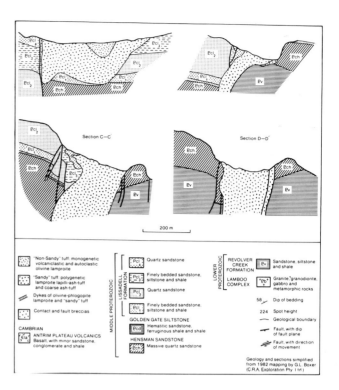

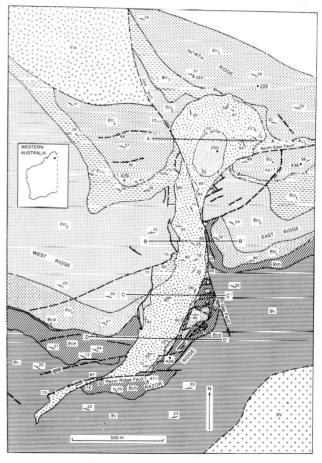

Figure 9-4. Geologic map and cross section showing rock units, structure, and location of Argyle mine in Western Australia.

History and Production of Diamonds in Australia

Secondary or alluvial diamonds, largely from alluvial gold workings, have been known in Australia since 1851, when diamonds were found at Bathurst in New South Wales. Between that time and 1922, more than 200,000 carats of diamonds were produced from the Copetown, Bingara, and Cudgegong fields, all in New South Wales (McNevin, 1977). These New South Wales fields have seen little production since the 1920s. Interest in diamond exploration had a resurgence in Australia, particularly in southeastern Australia, in the 1960s, but the results were relatively insignificant.

Even though diamonds were first discovered with gold in 1895 in Western Australia, near the town of Nullagine in the Pilbara region some 800 km from Kimberley, little interest in exploration developed in this area of the country. By the end of the 1960s, interest in the area had slowly developed. The first exploration work for diamonds in the Kimberley region of Western Australia began in 1967 and included three major entities: Stockdale Prospecting (DeBeers), Oilmin N. L. Consortium, and Stellar Minerals, N. L. Between 1967 and 1971, nine small diamonds were recovered from the area, but further work failed to find any additional stones or indications of a source.

In July 1972, the Kalumbura Joint Venture was established to prospect for diamonds north of 19° south latitude in the Kimberley region. By October 1973, the Kalumbura Joint Venture discovered several small diamonds in the King George River area in north Kimberley, and further, more vigorous exploration was encouraged. Exploration activities took a dramatic boost in February 1976, when CRA joined the exploration consortium and the Kalumbura Joint Venture became the Ashton Joint Venture. By the end of 1977, a very large pipe was discovered at Ellendale in West Kimberley, and about 12 small gem diamonds up to 0.1 carats were recovered. A small recovery plant was constructed at the site. In 1978 a concentrated effort was put forth on the Ellendale area. Even though 46 lamproitic pipes were delineated and 60 to 90 percent of the diamonds recovered were of gem quality, the deposit was considered uneconomic at this time. It did encourage more exploration, however. By the summer of 1979, exploration activity began to center on the Smoke Creek area some 25 km east of the Great Northern Highway. On August 28, 1979, the Perth laboratory reported finding two diamonds in a sample collected in this area. The next day they noted four more stones, followed by five stones 2 days later. In the 3-day period, they found

11 diamonds, all from the Smoke Creek drainage. In September, a concentrated effort began to follow the Smoke Creek drainage upstream until, on October 2, 1979, they discovered the diamond's source, the Argyle (AK1) pipe. In 1981 alluvial diamonds were found in the Limestone Creek drainage on the southeast side of the Argyle pipe. This deposit has estimated reserves of 1.6 million tons yielding an estimated 3.4 carats per metric ton.

Early, limited scale production began in January 1983 with the Smoke Creek Alluvial deposit. The Smoke Creek gravels totaled an estimated 580,000 metric tons, with an estimated yield of 4.6 carats per ton. In its first year of production, 6,154,639 carats of diamond, valued at more than $60 million, were recovered.

Full-scale mining and production began in early 1986. The Argyle Diamond Mines Pty. Limited is utilizing the open-pit method at the Argyle mine (Fig. 9-5), with ore dumped from 77-ton trucks onto a stockpile to await processing in the state-of-the-art treatment plant. The treatment plant is designed to process 3 million tons of lamproite ore a year (Fig. 9-6). The topography around the mine is exceedingly rugged, and an estimated 20 million tons of overburden had to be stripped from the pipe surface before operations could proceed. In its first year it yielded 29.2 million carats of diamond and became the largest single producer of diamond in the world today. Unfortunately, only about 5 percent were of gem-quality, accounting for about 3 percent of the world's gem-quality diamonds. Approximately 40 percent are considered "cheap gem," and the remaining 55 percent are industrial-grade diamonds. In terms of richness, the Argyle pipe is almost five times richer than the world's average, yielding nearly 7 carats per ton of ore. Proven ore reserves for the pipe are estimated to be 61 million tons, with an average yield of an incredible 6.8 carats per metric ton. A further estimated 14 million tons with a yield of 6.1 carats per metric ton have been classified as "probable reserve." Given current economic factors, this would guarantee the production of the Argyle pipe for at least 20 years.

Geology of the Argyle Pipe

The regional geology of the East Kimberley area has been described in detail by Dow and Gemuts (1969). The Argyle pipe is geologically situated in a major tectonic feature known as the Halls Creek Mobile Zone, a 400-km-long, north-northeast-trending belt of deformed Precambrian metamorphic, igneous, and sedimentary rocks, overlain in part by Paleozoic sedimentary and volcanic rocks.

Figure 9-5. The open-pit Argyle mine. Photo by Brian Stevenson. Courtesy of Argyle Diamond Sales.

Figure 9-6. The diamond-recovery plant located adjacent to the Argyle mine. Photo by Brian Stevenson. Courtesy of Argyle Diamond Sales.

According to Jaques and associates (1986), the Halls Creek Mobile Zone is particularly significant because it separates the older cratons of the Stuart Block and the Kimberley Block and is about 60 km wide. Its boundaries are delineated by two major faults: the Halls Creek fault on the east and the Greenvale fault on the west. The location of the lamproite intrusions, including the Argyle pipe, is believed to be strongly controlled by the evolution of the Halls Creek Mobile Zone, particularly faulting. Its history has, therefore, been of great interest. The most important study of the structure and evolution of this tectonic feature was by Hancock and Rutland (1984). They concluded that the evolution of the Halls Creek Mobile Zone was basically a series of extensions and compressions during Proterozoic times.

The Argyle pipe intruded two major sedimentary rock formations that are exposed in its vicinity: the Revolver Creek formation of early Proterozoic age and the Carr Boyd group of late Proterozoic age. The Revolver Creek formation consists of a basal unit of amygdaloidal basalt overlain by an alternating sequence of sandstone, siltstone, and shale. The formation is exposed south and west of the Argyle pipe and forms the base of the Matsu Range. Unconformably overlying the Revolver Creek formation and forming the main portion of the Matsu Range is the Carr Boyd group. This group consists of the Hensman sandstone, the Golden Gate siltstone, and the Lissadell formation of siltstone and shale.

The Argyle pipe occupies most of the small valley floor at the headwaters of Smoke Creek. The valley itself owes its existence to the preferential erosion of the relatively soft lamproite of the pipe over the sediments of the Revolver Creek formation and the Carr Boyd group. The pipe itself is an elongated body about 2 km long in a north-south direction and varying in width from about 500 meters at the bowl-shaped north end and narrowing to 150 meters further south. The pipe's surface exposure is almost 50 hectares.

Petrographically, the Argyle pipe is an olivine lamproite. The pipe consists predominantly of a volcanic sandy lapilli tuff containing up to 60 percent rounded quartz grains derived from the surrounding country rock, together with clasts of lamproite. The center of the northern end—the bowl of the pipe—is composed of a nonsandy tuff totally free of detrital quartz.

The age of the Argyle pipe has been determined by the Rb-Sr whole rock method (Pidgeon and Smith, in prep.) of both the lamproite and the shale horizons above and below the Lissadell formation of the Carr Boyd group immediately adjacent to the pipe (Bofinger, 1967). The ages of the two rock types agree well. The lamproite age was determined to be between 1,048 and 1,253 million years. The adjacent shales, which were intruded by the lamproite, were determined to be between 1,057 and 1,158 million years.

Characteristics of Argyle Diamonds

Hall and Smith's (1984) detailed study of the Argyle diamonds noted that the average stone weight is less than 0.1 carat, although stones up to almost 17 carats have been found. The relatively small average weight may be due to the strong resorption of the diamonds. Irregular "resorbed" shapes are predominant. Typically, the Argyle stones are fractured, strongly resorbed dodecahedra or combinations of dodecahedra and octahedra. Deeply etched channels are also characteristic. Minor amounts of macles and crystal aggregates have been noted, and no cubic crystals have been observed.

As noted earlier, only about 5 percent of the Argyle diamonds are of gem quality (Fig. 9-7), with about 40 percent designated as cheap gem and the remaining 55 percent as individual grade. Almost 80 percent of the diamonds from Argyle are brown, and most of the remaining 20 percent are yellow and colorless. Very significant, however, are the rare but economically important pink diamonds that are bringing Argyle fame. Green diamonds are also found occasionally.

Graphite is the most common mineral inclusion in Argyle diamonds. Other minerals noted by Hall and Smith (1984) are almandine-pyrope garnets, diopside, kyanite, and rutile. Hofer (1985) also noted a clear mineral that he assumed to be olivine. Henry Meyer (personal communication) also noted chrome pyrope-garnet, spinel, and clinopyroxene.

Hofer (1985) undertook detailed gemological studies of the Argyle diamonds. After studying a sample of 138 pink diamonds ranging in weight from 0.04 to 2.65 carats, he concluded that the Argyle diamonds typically had a "smoky purplish pink" body color. Spectral analysis revealed a Cape absorption line at 415 nm as well as a weak "smudge" at about 520 to 580 nm. Under long-wave ultraviolet radiation, the Argyle diamonds fluoresced from very weak to very strong blue; under shortwave ultraviolet radiation, they fluoresced either not at all or moderately blue. Hofer (1985) also noted that stones that fluoresced strongly blue under long-wave exhibited yellow phosphorescence under magnification; he also noted distinct

Figure 9-7. Assortment of Argyle diamonds. Photo by Harold and Erica Van Pelt.

color zoning along "grain lines." Some of the most characteristic features of the Argyle pink diamonds are the irregular "frosted" cleavage cracks and a pitted surface on narrow voids and channels on the surface of the stones. Other gemological properties studied by Hofer (1985) appear to be uncharacteristic.

The Argyle diamonds are sold through Argyle Diamond Sales Ltd., which markets the majority of them through the Central Selling Organization (CSO) on behalf of the CRA Ltd. and the Ashton Mining Group (Fig. 9-8). All gem diamonds and 75 pecent of the cheap gems and industrials are sold through the CSO, and Argyle Diamond Sales retains 25 percent of the cheap gem and industrial diamonds for sale to other customers. Argyle Diamond Sales has an overseas sales office in Antwerp, in addition to its headquarters office in Perth. Significantly, Argyle Diamond Sales has also established a small-scale pilot diamond-cutting factory in Perth to test the economic viability of a much larger plant in the future.

Figure 9-8. This 3.53 ct. blue diamond, set in a ring, is surrounded by 36 Australian pink diamonds with a 2.64 ct. total weight. The 0.72 ct. intense purple-pink, heart-shaped diamond in the necklace is also from Australia. Collection of R. Esmerian, Inc., New York. Photo by Harold and Erica Van Pelt.

REFERENCES

Argyle Diamond Mines Joint Venture Project Briefing. 1985. Private Report. 95 pages.

Atkinson, W. J. 1987. The exploration and development of Australian diamond. *Industrial Diamond Review* (January):1–8.

Atkinson, W. J., F. E. Hughes, and C. B. Smith. 1982. A review of the kimberlitic rocks of Western Australia (abstract). *Terra Cognita* 2:204.

Atkinson, W. J., F. E. Hughes, and C. B. Smith. 1984a. A review of the kimberlitic rocks of Western Australia, 195–224. In J. Kornprobst, ed., *Kimberlites 1: Kimberlites and Related Rocks*. Elsevier, Amsterdam.

Atkinson, W. J., C. B. Smith, and G. L. Boxer. 1984b. The discovery and evaluation of the Ellendale and Argyle lamproite diamond deposits, Kimberley Region, Western Australia. Denver, SME Conference, 1984.

Bofinger, V. M. 1967. Geochronology of the east Kimberley area of Western Australia. Ph.D. Thesis (unpublished), Australian National University.

Boxer, G. L., C. B. Smith, and V. Lorenz. 1986. Geology and volcanology of Argyle AK 1 lamproite diatreme. 4th Int. Kimberlite Conf. (Perth), Extended Abstracts.

Boyd, F. R., and L. W. Finger. 1976. Homogeneity of minerals in mantle rocks from Lesotho. *Ann. Rept. Dir. Geophys. Lab.* 1975–76:519–528.

Clement, C. R., and E. M. W. Skinner. 1979. A textural-genetic classification of kimberlite rocks. Kimberlite Symp. III, Univ. Cambridge, 4 pages.

Clement, C. R., E. M. W. Skinner, and B. H. Scott Smith. 1977. Kimberlite redefined. 2d International Kimberlite Conf., Santa Fe, Abstracts (unpublished).

Clement, C. R., E. M. W. Skinner, and B. H. Scott Smith. 1984. Kimberlite redefined. *Jour. Geol.* 92:223–228.

Dow, D. B., and I. Gemuts. 1969. *Geology of Kimberley Region, Western Australia: The East Kimberley* Australia BMR, Bull. 200.

Ferguson, J., and J. W. Sheraton, 1979. Petrogenesis of kimberlitic rocks and associated xenoliths of southeastern Australia, 140–160. In F. R. Boyd and H. O. A. Meyer, eds., *Kimberlites, Diatremes, and Diamonds: (1) Their Geology, Petrology, and Geochemistry.* American Geophysical Union, Washington, D.C. 400 pages.

Fumey, P. 1985. Le pipe d'Argyle. *Revue de Gemmologie a.f.g.* 2:18–20.

Geach, C. L. 1986. Diamond Exploration in Western Australia. *Geology Today* 2(1):16–20.

Groom, F. F. 1896. Report of a visit to Bullagine, Pibara district, to examine the country reported to be diamond yielding. *West Australia Dept. Mines Ann. Rept.* (1895): 27.

Guilbert, J. M., and C. F. Park, Jr. 1986. *The Geology of Ore Deposits.* W. H. Freeman and Company, New York. 985 pages.

Hall, A. E., and C. B. Smith. 1984. Lamproite diamonds: Are they different? 167–212. In J. E. Glover and P. G. Harris, eds., *Kimberlite Occurrence and Origin.* University of Western Australia Geology Dept., Publ. 8.

Hancock, S. L., and R. W. R. Rutland. 1984. Tectonics of an early Proterozoic geosuture: The Halls Creek orogenic subprovince, northern Australia. *Jour. Geodynamics* 1:387–432.

Hardman, E. T. 1884. Report of the geology of the Kimberley district, Western Australia. *West Australia Parlt. Papers* (1884): 31.

Hawthorne, J. B. 1975. Model of a kimberlite pipe. *Phys. Chem. Earth* 9:1–15.

Hofer, S. C. 1985. Pink Diamonds from Australia. *Gems & Gemology* 21 (3):147–155.

Jaques, A. L., J. Ferguson, and C. B. Smith. 1984. Kimberlites in Australia, 227–274. In J. E. Glover and P. G. Harris, *Kimberlite Occurrence and Origin.* University of Western Australia Geology Dept., Publ. 8.

Jaques, A. L., J. D. Lewis, and C. B. Smith. 1986. *The Kimberlites and Lamproites of Western Australia.* Geological Survey of Western Australia Bulletin 132. 268 pages.

Kennedy, G. C., and B. E. Nordlie. 1968. The genesis of diamond deposits. *Econ. Geol.* 63:495–503.

McNevin, A. A. 1977. Diamonds in New South Wales. New South Wales Geological Survey, *Min. Res. Bull.* 42.

Meakins, A. 1983. Geology and genesis of the Argyle alluvial diamond deposits, Kimberley region, Western Australia, 54–56. R. Davy, C. R. M. Butt, and T. A. Ballinger, eds., In *Geochemical Exploration in Arid and Deeply Weathered Environments: Geochemistry and Genesis of Ore Deposits Associated with Weathering.* Assoc. Expl. Geochemists, Regional Meeting, Perth, 1983, Abstracts.

O'Neill, H. St. C., A. L. Jaques, C. B. Smith, and J. Moon. (In preparation.) Diamond-bearing peridotite xenoliths from the Argyle (AK1) pipe: 4th Int. Kimberlite Conf., Perth, Abstract volume.

Pidgeon, R. T., and C. B. Smith. (In preparation.) The ages of kimberlite and lamproite emplacement in Western Australia. 4th Int. Kimberlite Conf., Perth, Abstracts volume.

Skinner, E. M. W., and C. R. Clement. 1979. Mineralogical classification of southern African kimberlites, 129–139. In F. R. Boyd and H. O. A. Meyer, eds., *Kimberlites, Diatremes, and Diamonds: (1) Their Geology, Petrology, and Geochemistry.* American Geophysical Union, Washington, D.C. 400 pages.

INDEX